For David and Arnie.

Cruising Cuisine

FOR HOME ENTERTAINING

HORS D'OEUVRES AND APPETIZERS VOLUME ONE

BY ELENA VAKHRENOVA

DESIGN BY BONNIE CARTER

PHOTOGRAPHY BY ELENA VAKHRENOVA

Permissions Department
Cruising Cuisine for Home Entertaining, Inc.
13041 NW 3rd Street, Plantation, FL 33325.

Library of Congress Cataloging-in-Publication Data
Vakhrenova, Elena.
   Cruising cuisine for home entertaining. Volume one,
 Hors d'oeuvres and appetizers / by Elena Vakhrenova ;
 design by Bonnie Carter; photography by Elena
 Vakhrenova.
     p. cm.
     ISBN 0-9722422-0-1

   1. Appetizers. 2. Cookery, Marine.   I. Title.

TX740.V35 2003   641.8'12
                        QBI02-200865

Printed in Singapore

First Printing

www.cruising-cuisine.com

ACKNOWLEDGMENTS

They say that life is like an open book. My life brought me to the page where I found *Cruising Cuisine for Home Entertaining* and the many people that made this book happen. Each and every one of them deserves my gratitude for their support along this journey.

Among them is my husband who is always excited about all my dreams and plans. I would like to thank him for believing in me, for his invaluable experience in writing and marketing, and for his help and support in everything I do. I will never be more grateful than for those dinners you took me out to every time I was exhausted from cooking and shooting pictures!

I would also like to thank Mary Ellis, my neighbor and friend whom I found shortly after my arrival in America. Her excitement for our cooking classes and this book kept me going. Mary, your help in food editing and most importantly, your friendship is invaluable.

I cannot imagine a cookbook without photography, one of the most exciting and difficult steps in publishing. My deepest thanks to Doug Castanedo, a wonderful friend and professional photographer, who taught me the basics of food photography.

My special thanks to Natasha Mullin, for her advice and professional editing; Linda Schultes, for her amazing spirit, excitement and help in understanding printing and production; Andrea Corman, for her encouragement and help in food editing; and Bonnie Carter for her beautiful design.

Thanks to my first cooking class students: Joyce Giacoma, Donna Rudolf, Catherine Robinson, Denise Benson, Beth Lehn, Sherry Donovan, Catherine Totoiu, Elizabeth Perez, Jeannette Carter, Michal Ann Swofford, Patti Barre, BJ Hansen, Brenda Falsone, Leslie Barber and Mary Ballback.

And last but not least, my thanks to our neighbors at Lago Mar: Elena and John Moreland, Mary and John Ellis, Karen and Bob Cozzi, Valerie and Bob Rossi, Cindy and Greg Calvert – all of whom had more fun than anybody else in tasting the food and giving their advice. You are the best support any neighbor can dream of. Ready for new tasting? I am!

CONTENTS

INTRODUCTION

 CRUISING CUISINE'S ORIGINS — Cruising has been with me since I was about six years old. Maybe that is because my parents met on the cruise ship where my father worked as a cook and my mother served as a bartender. Or maybe it is because my father's company allowed him to take his family on his ship several times a year. On one cruise, I remember my father trying to keep me busy by sending me "to help his cooks to cook," and how one of the cooks, laughing, placed me in front of the cooking range and we made Russian blini for French passengers. Thereafter, my childhood cruises consisted of making my daily rounds: checking out the bars, playing in the casino before it opened, exploring all the "For Crew Only" staircases, and spending time in the most exciting and important place on the ship, the galley.

Raised on the Black Sea in Odessa, I led a life that revolved around the experiences of cruise ships and cooking. When my father came ashore, I worked at his restaurant as a "Jack of all trades." Later, I became the chef at a five-star government hotel. My mother seemed happy with my choices until the day I came home and announced that I would embark on a ship in three days! With tears in her eyes, she gave me her blessing and admitted that her time on ships was the best time of her life.

At 22, and speaking only Russian, I boarded a 600-passenger, 240-crew member cruise ship catering to American passengers. During the next eight years, I learned six other languages and mastered numerous positions from captain's stewardess to assistant hotel manager to cruise director. And whether I was cruising at sea or on the majestic inland rivers of Europe, there was one thing that always meant the most to me: the time spent with shipmates, passengers, friends and family enjoying the simple act of sharing a meal.

Cruising Cuisine for Home Entertaining is a tribute to those memories, and to the good times.

TODAY'S CRUISING CUISINE – Since that period of my life, I have found that people tend to fall into two categories: those who cruise and those who think about it. Chances are good that at the last party you attended, someone was either talking about a cruise they had taken or about the one they were planning. And the rest of us? From coast to coast, we all ask the same question at every gathering where cruising is mentioned: How was the food?

Most of us hear "cruise" and immediately see images of gracious dining and incredible buffets. Our senses are filled with the expectations of food that appeals to the eye as well as to the palate. Subtle aromas, a dish that tempts the eye from across the room. "What is that?" he asks the woman seated next to him. "May I have a bite?" she says quietly to her husband.

While the quality and variety of food and its presentation may vary from one cruise line to the next, there is one universal truth for most of us: we don't eat like this at home! *Cruising Cuisine for Home Entertaining* is about bringing a little cruise ship style to your home entertainment. Before long, your friends and family will be talking about your last party with the same excitement they talk about their last cruise!

Before we cast off, here are some basics about how I have organized the selection of hors d'oeuvres and appetizers in this book. The cruise industry looks at itself in three generally accepted categories, both for quality and variety as well as presentation. I have adopted this system by categorizing the selections as: Contemporary, Premium and Luxury – each designed to reflect the style of the party you are planning, and each representative of the style of entertaining you might find aboard the distinguished ships mentioned in each grouping.

As you turn the page, think "**Bon Voyage!**"

CONTEMPORARY

Think of Carnival Cruise Line and Norwegian Cruise Line, and you are thinking contemporary cruising. The style is casual, the mood is fun. On board you will find a mix of fellow passengers from mature to families with young children. Cruise almost anywhere in the world from less than a week to more than two, and from the warm waters of the Caribbean and Mediterranean to the cooler climates of Alaska and Scandinavia.

On board you will find a dining experience on par with most high quality shore-based restaurants. When compared to other cruising categories, some might perceive the dining experience as less elaborate because contemporary cruising has gained its current popularity by emphasizing the ship as a fabulous floating resort. You will find an amazing variety of on-board activities, and on newer ships, multiple dining venues, specialty restaurants, and 24-hour buffet service. With a focus on presenting a high quality main course, the choice of hors d'oeuvres and appetizers may seem less complex when compared to other cruising categories.

This section offers a variety of contemporary-style hors d'oeuvres and appetizers that are easy to prepare and fun to serve. You will find them a perfect accompaniment for late afternoon or an early evening get together, as part of an outdoor barbecue, or as a nice prelude to a simple family dinner.

GREEK TZATZIKI

The captain of my first ship was Greek, so it is little wonder how I learned this famous recipe. Always a favorite, tzatziki is both a great party pleaser and a traditional accompaniment to lamb. We like it with pita bread, but especially with fresh baked French bread. For better results, refrigerate for at least 6 hours before serving.

Line a medium strainer with cheese cloth. Place over a medium bowl and spoon in yogurt. Drain at room temperature for 2 hours.

Place yogurt in a medium bowl. Add chopped cucumber, dill, garlic, olive oil, lemon juice and season with salt and pepper. Mix gently until blended. Chill in refrigerator for 6 to 10 hours for flavors to meld.

Transfer to a small bowl, garnish and serve.

MAKES 4 to 6 servings
PREPARATION 15 minutes
DRAINING 2 hours
CHILLING 6 to 10 hours
SPECIAL EQUIPMENT cheese cloth
GARNISH freshly ground pepper, fresh dill

1 container (32 ounces) plain yogurt

½ English hothouse cucumber, peeled and finely chopped

½ cup chopped fresh dill

5 garlic cloves, minced

1 tablespoon extra virgin olive oil

1 tablespoon fresh lemon juice

Salt and freshly ground pepper to taste

CHICKEN SALAD CANAPÉS

This simple chicken salad made a couple of hours ahead is a great base for cocktail hour hors d'oeuvres. Be ready to answer questions like, "This is good...but...what is it?" It might help to have a story like "During my last cruise to Indonesia, we stopped at Bau Bau where the local tribal chief suggested an unusual..."

In a large bowl, mix the chicken, eggs, onion and mayonnaise with garlic powder, salt and pepper.

Cut the crust off the bread, then cut each slice into 4 squares or triangles. Top each with ½ tablespoon chicken salad.

Transfer to a serving platter, garnish and serve.

MAKES 20 to 24 canapés
PREPARATION 35 to 40 minutes
GARNISH bell pepper, fresh dill

1 cup finely chopped boiled or roasted chicken meat

2 eggs, hard-boiled and finely chopped

½ small onion, finely chopped

2 tablespoons mayonnaise

Garlic powder, salt and pepper to taste

6 bread slices, ¼ to ½ inch thick

TIP In lieu of bread or in addition to, use any favorite cracker or flatbread for a base.

MINI QUICHE LORRAINE

You will navigate with many options when you make our mini quiches. You can make them ahead and freeze, or bake the shells a few days ahead, leaving the filling and baking for the last day. As you cruise your way through this recipe, don't be afraid to go off course and discover something of your own!

Preheat oven to 400°F.

TARTLETS Unfold pastry on a lightly floured surface. Roll out each pie crust into a 12-inch round making the dough as thin as possible. Using a cutter, cut out 12 rounds per pie crust. Pierce each with a fork in 5 or 6 different places. Transfer each round to an ungreased muffin pan and press the dough to the bottom and sides with your fingers, slightly fluting the edges to form a quiche 'flower' shell. Line each shell with aluminum foil and fill with ceramic pie weights.

Bake 8 to 10 minutes or until lightly golden but not completely baked. Set aside and cool before taking each shell out of the form.

FILLING Preheat large skillet over low heat and sauté bacon until almost crisp. Remove all but 1 tablespoon of bacon drippings. In the same skillet, add onions and sauté until light brown. Set aside to cool.

In a medium bowl, lightly beat the eggs. Add sour cream, parsley, cheese, salt, pepper and nutmeg. Gently mix.

TO BAKE MINI QUICHES Preheat oven to 350°F.

Remove cold quiche shells from muffin forms. Place on a baking sheet. In each shell, spoon ¼ teaspoon bacon mixture. Top it with ¼ teaspoon cheese and gently pour 1 tablespoon of egg mixture over bacon and cheese.

Bake 15 to 20 minutes or until a fork when inserted comes out clean. Transfer to a platter and serve immediately.

MAKES 24 mini quiches
PREPARATION 65 to 70 minutes
COOKING 50 to 55 minutes
SPECIAL EQUIPMENT 3-inch diameter cutter or glass; ceramic pie weights or dried beans; 2 mini-muffin trays, 12 muffin forms each, 8½ x 11 inches; aluminum foil or parchment paper cut into twenty four 2½-inch squares

1 package 9-inch pie crust, 2 in the pack (Pillsbury or other)

1 package (8 ounces) bacon, finely chopped

1 large onion, finely chopped

3 eggs

½ cup sour cream

3 tablespoons finely chopped fresh parsley

½ cup grated Swiss cheese

Salt, pepper, nutmeg to taste

SAVORY RUSSIAN BLINI

Most of us think of caviar and blini in the same sentence, but at home in Odessa, blini are used for everything and served at any time. For breakfast they are eaten with sour cream and jam or honey as a topping. For lunch or dinner, blini can be stuffed with meat and for dessert, white cheese and raisins.

BLINI In a medium bowl, whisk eggs until smooth. Add milk and whisk until combined. To avoid lumps, add flour by sprinkling it over the bowl surface, a little at a time. Incorporate well after each addition. Mix in sugar and salt, and add water little by little until the batter is perfectly smooth.

Preheat skillet over medium heat and brush with oil. When very hot, pour a ladle half filled with batter slowly around the edge, quickly rotating so that the batter covers the bottom of the skillet in a very thin layer. Pour excess batter back into the bowl. Cook the blini on one side until golden brown. Transfer to a plate and continue cooking the rest of the blini until all batter is used.

STUFFING Bring 4 cups of water to a boil. Carefully place the pork in the salted water. Cover and return to a boil. Reduce the heat and boil until cooked, about 30 minutes. Transfer meat to a plate, set aside and let cool.

In a skillet, preheat 1 tablespoon oil over medium heat and sauté the onions until golden.

Cut the pork into approximately 1-inch pieces. In a food processor, pulse the meat and onions (with the oil) until coarsely ground. Season with salt and pepper.

TO FOLD BLINI IN 'ENVELOPE' OR 'BURRITO' STYLE Place blini on a working surface with browned side up. Spoon approximately 1 tablespoon of filling on blini, 1 inch from the edge. Fold this edge over the filling, then overlap with left and right edges and roll over. Transfer to the plate and repeat with remaining blini.

In a large skillet, preheat remaining oil over medium heat and sauté stuffed blini on both sides until golden brown. Transfer to a plate, top with 1 teaspoon of sour cream and serve immediately.

MAKES 20 to 24 blini
PREPARATION 55 to 60 minutes
COOKING 1½ to 2 hours
SPECIAL EQUIPMENT 8- or 10-inch skillet

2 eggs

2 cups milk

3 cups all-purpose flour

½ teaspoon sugar

½ teaspoon salt

2 cups water

½ cup sunflower or vegetable oil

½ pound pork shoulder (boneless)

1 large onion, finely chopped

Salt and pepper to taste

TIP Add some flour if the blini are too thin and difficult to turn or add some water or milk if the blini are too thick.

Blini can be folded ahead and kept refrigerated up to 24 hours leaving a quick sautéing before serving.

GARLIC & SHRIMP APPETIZER

With this appetizer, your guests will never "kiss and tell" – everybody will know from the fragrance of garlic. There is nothing better than dipping the crispy crust of freshly baked sourdough or French bread into the hot garlic oil while eating the shrimp. This is appetizer 'heaven' for garlic and shrimp lovers, and those who love them!

Preheat broiler to 450°F.

Make a cut along the back of shrimp and remove vein. Wash under cold running water and dry with paper towels. Place shrimp in a single layer in a large oven-safe dish. Pour olive oil over the shrimp and sprinkle with minced garlic.

Broil on an upper rack until shrimp are pink and opaque, 6 to 10 minutes. It is not necessary to turn shrimp while cooking. Watch carefully as shrimp can overcook very easily.

Sprinkle shrimp with chives, salt and pepper and serve immediately.

MAKES 4 servings
PREPARATION 15 to 20 minutes
COOKING 6 to 10 minutes
GARNISH fresh lemon

½ **pound raw jumbo or king shrimp (shelled)**
½ **cup extra virgin olive oil**
14 **garlic cloves, minced**
¼ **cup chives, finely chopped**
Salt and cracked pepper to taste

FRENCH OLIVIER HORS D'OEUVRES

During a cruise on the Rhône, I discovered a French vegetable salad called "Olivier" and have adapted it to create a unique presentation. You will find it an attractive addition to your party as a buffet salad, and the dish goes over well at barbeques. We do not recommend skipping any of the vegetables but you can use any kind of ham or roasted or boiled chicken.

Finely dice the potato, carrot, egg, pickles and ham.

In a large bowl, toss diced vegetables, egg and ham with green peas and onions. Add mayonnaise, salt and pepper to taste and toss gently.

Chill in the refrigerator for at least 1 hour and serve cold.

Cut one inch off the bottom of the endive, separate the leaves, and keep in cold water until ready to assemble.

Dry with paper towel and spoon about 1 teaspoon of mixture onto each leaf. Garnish and serve immediately.

MAKES 16 to 20 hors d'oeuvres
PREPARATION 40 to 50 minutes
COOKING 55 to 60 minutes
CHILLING 1 to 6 hours
GARNISH chopped fresh dill

1 large potato, boiled and peeled

1 carrot, boiled and peeled

1 egg, hard-boiled and peeled

2 medium pickles

3 ounces Boar's Head ham

¼ cup green peas, canned

**1 small onion, chopped
(or ½ cup of green scallions, chopped)**

½ cup light mayonnaise

Salt and pepper to taste

4 small Belgian endives

CRAB SALAD APPETIZER

On any cruise, presentation is everything! Here you will find a delightful crab salad made into a whimsical "toadstool," reminiscent of something found in the deep forest! If you are less adventurous or your guests are not intrepid explorers, feel free to serve the salad on a cracker or in a serving bowl.

Peel eggs and cut off the top quarter of the egg. Carefully scoop the yolks and set aside, reserving the egg whites.

In a small bowl, whisk 1 tablespoon of mayonnaise, mustard and lemon juice. Add the crabmeat, yolks, carrots, chives, lemon zest, salt and pepper and toss gently.

Stuff each egg with 1 to 2 teaspoons of crab stuffing and stand the eggs on a serving platter. Cut a small slice from the bottom if easier to stand. Cover with plastic wrap and chill in the refrigerator for 1 hour.

To make the caps, make 2 vertical cuts on opposite sides of the tomato stem. Place the tomato on top of the egg.

Dip a toothpick in mayonnaise and make 8 to 14 dots on the "head" of each "toadstool."

Garnish the platter and serve cold.

MAKES 12 appetizers
PREPARATION 80 to 90 minutes
COOKING 15 to 20 minutes
CHILLING 1 hour
SPECIAL EQUIPMENT 1 toothpick
GARNISH finely sliced lettuce

12 eggs, hard-boiled

2 tablespoons mayonnaise or sour cream

1 teaspoon Dijon mustard

1/2 teaspoon fresh lemon juice

4 ounces fresh or canned lump crabmeat (well-drained if canned)

1/2 tablespoon grated fresh carrot

1/2 tablespoon finely chopped chives

1/2 teaspoon fresh lemon zest

Salt and pepper to taste

3 to 5 small to medium, round tomatoes

TIP Stuffed eggs can be chilled in the refrigerator prior to serving leaving 10 minutes to assemble.

ITALIAN EGGPLANT BRUSCHETTA ON CROSTINI

The secret to great tasting bruschetta is not only the topping, but how the bread is prepared. In this *Cruising Cuisine* recipe, you can create perfect crostini by first tossing the bread in Italian herb seasoning and then toasting in extra virgin olive oil. This "Taste of Italy" appetizer is perfect for any occasion and your guests will be dreaming of the brightly colored, sun-drenched Mediterranean with every bite.

Cut the ends from the eggplant. Clean and remove the seeds from the bell pepper.

Place eggplant, tomato, pepper and onion in a large pot. Pour the oil and vinegar over the vegetables. Add bay leaves, peppercorns and garlic cloves. Cover and bring to a boil. Reduce heat to low and simmer the vegetables until soft and immersed in liquid, about 60 minutes. Set aside and stir in chopped parsley. Let cool.

Remove the bay leaves and garlic. Chop the vegetables and transfer to a bowl. Cover with plastic wrap and chill in the refrigerator before serving. Prior to serving, separate the leaves of fresh cilantro and combine with vegetables.

In a large skillet, preheat oil over medium heat. Toast bread until golden, about 2 minutes on each side.

Place about one tablespoon of bruschetta on each crostini.

Serve cold.

MAKES 18 to 20 hors d'oeuvres
PREPARATION 30 to 40 minutes
COOKING 55 to 65 minutes

1 medium eggplant

1 red bell pepper

1 medium or large tomato, cored

1 medium onion, outer skin removed

1 cup extra virgin olive oil

1 cup distilled white vinegar

2 bay leaves

1 teaspoon whole black peppercorns

2 garlic cloves

½ cup chopped fresh parsley

½ cup fresh cilantro

6 bread or baguette slices, ¼ to ½ inch thick

Olive oil for toasting

STUFFED CHAMPIGNON CAPS

The difference between a mushroom and a champignon is attitude. In *Cruising Cuisine*, **our attitude definitely favors the champignon as one of the favorite ingredients in any cuisine. You can create a versatile appetizer with a simple stuffing made from whatever you have in your refrigerator — from cream cheese to ricotta and goat cheese, or tomatoes, basil and mozzarella, or Swiss or Monterey Jack cheese combined with herbs.**

Wash the champignons under cold running water and dry on paper towels. Remove the stems from the champignons and reserve for stuffing.

In a medium skillet, heat the oil over low heat. Add chopped onion and sauté until lightly browned. Add chopped mushroom stems, bay leaf, salt and pepper and sauté until stems are cooked and brown. Set aside to cool to room temperature.

Preheat oven to 350°F.

Transfer the stuffing to a small bowl, add grated cheese and mix the ingredients gently. Place champignons on a baking sheet and stuff each cap with about 1 tablespoon of stuffing distributing evenly into a mound. Bake about 25 to 30 minutes or until the tops become golden brown.

Transfer to a serving platter and serve warm or at room temperature.

MAKES 12 hors d'oeuvres
PREPARATION 10 to 15 minutes
COOKING 30 to 40 minutes

12 large champignons
1 tablespoon olive oil
1 small onion, finely chopped
1 bay leaf
Salt and pepper to taste
3 tablespoons grated Swiss cheese

TIP Stuff the caps up to 12 hours ahead of baking.

TUNA HORS D' OEUVRES

Not every night aboard ship is a five-star feast. But we can still make something extra special from even the simplest of ingredients. Tuna salad is a perfect tray-passed hors d'oeuvre when served on crackers or French bread rounds. Garnish with chopped fresh onion and dill and you will have them coming back for more! Note that the tuna in oil has a much better flavor than that in water. Tuna mixture can be made up to 6 hours ahead and kept refrigerated.

Use the lid of the can to drain excess oil.

In a food processor, blend the tuna, mayonnaise, salt and pepper until smooth.

Spoon about ½ tablespoon of tuna on each cracker, garnish and serve cold.

MAKES 10 to 12 hors d'oeuvres
PREPARATION 15 to 20 minutes
GARNISH finely chopped onion, fresh dill

1 can (6 ounces) light tuna or solid white albacore in oil

1 tablespoon mayonnaise

Salt and pepper to taste

10 to 12 crackers

TIP For a different presentation, arrange tuna on ½-inch slices of English hothouse cucumber. Or, serve this dish as a dip with crackers on the side. Simply mix blended tuna with fresh dill until combined. Transfer to a small bowl and sprinkle with chopped onion.

CREAMY GUACAMOLE

Let *Cruising Cuisine* dress up your guacamole by adding cilantro and making it creamy. You'll have a new version with a non-traditional attitude and a wonderful taste. This cool guacamole with a velvet texture can be made 2 to 3 hours ahead and kept covered with plastic wrap in the refrigerator. Add chopped tomatoes just before serving and serve with tortilla chips on the side.

Cut avocados in half and remove pits. Scoop flesh and transfer to the bowl of a food processor. Add lime juice, garlic, mayonnaise and cilantro and pulse until the mixture is pureed and smooth. Transfer to a serving bowl.

MAKES 4 servings
PREPARATION 8 to 10 minutes
GARNISH lime slices

2 ripe Hass avocados

¼ cup fresh lime juice

2 garlic cloves, chopped

1 tablespoon mayonnaise

1 cup fresh cilantro

½ cup chopped tomato (optional)

TIP Serve with colorful tortilla chips on the side. For a variation, stir in tomatoes and garnish with lime slices.

CRISPY TOASTS WITH PORTOBELLO MUSHROOM

If a visit to the Mediterranean is not on your cruising schedule this season, recreate the tastes of the Italian and French Riviera with this easy to prepare appetizer. Of course, eating at a café table with a blue and white striped umbrella will certainly help you practice for your next vacation.

Cut bread diagonally in two triangles. Brush a large skillet with olive oil and toast the bread slices over medium heat until nicely brown and crispy, 1 to 2 minutes on each side.

In a small skillet, heat 1 tablespoon of olive oil over medium heat. Sauté the mushrooms until cooked and the liquid has evaporated, about 2 minutes. Set aside and let cool to room temperature.

In a medium bowl, mix the mushrooms, tomatoes and basil.

Spread goat cheese to taste on each piece of bread and top with ½ to 1 tablespoon of mixture.

Transfer the toasts to a platter and serve immediately.

ITALIAN HERB SEASONING In a small bowl, mix all herbs until combined.

MAKES 10 toasts
PREPARATION 30 to 35 minutes
COOKING 7 to 10 minutes

5 bread slices, ¼ to ½ inch thick

2 tablespoons olive oil

¼ cup finely chopped portobello mushroom

¼ cup finely chopped tomato

¼ cup finely chopped fresh basil

2 to 3 ounces crumbled goat cheese

ITALIAN HERB SEASONING

¼ teaspoon dried oregano

¼ teaspoon dried marjoram

¼ teaspoon dried thyme

¼ teaspoon dried savory

¼ teaspoon dried basil

¼ teaspoon dried rosemary

¼ teaspoon dried sage

TIP Try using the Italian Herb Seasoning (recipe above) in addition to/or instead of basil.

SHRIMP SALAD CANAPÉS

This easy to prepare salad is light, refreshing, and reminiscent of sunny days lounging on deck by the pool. Not always a canapé, try serving as a luncheon salad or even as a dip for assorted flatbreads. For a variation, mix in sweet bell pepper or grated fresh carrot.

In a small bowl, whisk mayonnaise and sour cream until smooth.

Set aside 24 shrimp for garnishing.

In a medium bowl, combine the remaining shrimp, eggs, dill, chives, celery and season with salt and pepper. Add the mayonnaise mixture and stir gently. Cover with plastic wrap and chill in the refrigerator for 30 to 45 minutes.

Cut the crust from the bread, then cut each piece twice horizontally, making 4 squares or diagonally making triangles. Top each with ½ tablespoon of shrimp mixture.

Transfer to a serving platter, garnish and serve cold.

MAKES 24 canapés
PREPARATION 10 to 15 minutes
CHILLING 30 to 45 minutes
GARNISH fresh dill

¼ **cup mayonnaise**

¼ **cup sour cream**

1 pound cooked and peeled small cocktail shrimp

2 eggs, hard-boiled, peeled and chopped

½ **cup finely chopped fresh dill**

2 tablespoons chopped chives or green scallions

2 tablespoons finely chopped celery

Salt and pepper to taste

6 bread slices or crackers

ZUCCHINI, TOMATO & BASIL CANAPÉS

When you visit the sun-drenched ports of Italy, you will notice how often fresh vegetables become an entire meal for the locals. With this easy and convenient recipe, you will delight your vegetarian guests and surprise the rest! The best part is you can conveniently sauté the zucchini, and slice the tomatoes and bread when you have the time, quickly assembling the rest just before your party.

Slice zucchini in ¹/₂-inch slices and season with salt.

In a large skillet, preheat oil over medium heat. Dust each zucchini slice with flour and sauté both sides until golden brown and soft, about 30 seconds on the first side and 10 seconds on the second. Transfer sautéed slices to a plate, set aside and let cool.

In a small bowl, combine mayonnaise and garlic.

Slice the tomatoes in ¹/₂-inch slices.

Assemble the canapés by placing one zucchini on a slice of bread, smear with mayonnaise and top with a slice of tomato. Put a basil leaf in the center of the tomato and pierce the entire canapé with a toothpick. Arrange canapés on a platter and serve warm or at room temperature.

MAKES 24 canapés
PREPARATION 15 to 20 minutes
COOKING 2 to 5 minutes

1 small to medium zucchini

Salt to taste

3 tablespoons vegetable or olive oil

2 tablespoons all-purpose flour

1 tablespoon mayonnaise

1 garlic clove, minced

2 small plum tomatoes

24 French baguette slices, ¹/₂ inch thick

24 basil leaves

TIP Presentation is best if zucchini and tomato are the same diameter. Alternately, skewer vegetables with a frilly toothpick and serve with bread and crackers on the side allowing guests to eat with or without the base.

OLIVE TAPENADE

River cruises are a great way to see the heart of Europe and make amazing discoveries along the way. I encountered this delicious spread at a restaurant hidden in delightful Appeldoorn, a Rhine river city near Arnhem, Holland. An elegant appetizer, this dish adds an extra special touch to your dinner table when served in lieu of butter, especially with rustic full-bodied country breads.

In a food processor, pulse olives, sun-dried tomatoes, garlic, olive oil, salt and pepper until coarsely chopped or smooth like a paste. Add jalapeño sauce to taste.

Serve with fresh baked bread or crackers on the side.

MAKES 6 to 8 servings
PREPARATION 3 to 6 minutes

8 ounces Kalamata olives, pitted

1 tablespoon sun-dried tomatoes in oil, drained and coarsely chopped (optional)

2 garlic cloves, minced

½ cup extra virgin olive oil

Salt, pepper and Poblano Green Jalapeño Sauce (see mail order sources) to taste

TIP Allow flavors to fully develop by making tapenade in advance. Keep chilled in the refrigerator and use within 2 weeks.

PORTOBELLO CAPS WITH EGGPLANT, TOMATO, BASIL & MOZZARELLA

Your guests will think their ship has arrived in Italy when they taste your Italian portobello mushrooms stuffed with eggplant, tomato, basil and mozzarella. They may even sing *Oh Sole Mio* if you sprinkle the caps with Italian Herb Seasoning (see page 35) before baking. *Buon appetito*!

Cut eggplant in half horizontally and season with salt. Transfer to a plate and set aside for 15 to 30 minutes allowing the salt to remove the bitter moisture.

Clean the dark brown "gills" from the portobello caps. Lightly rinse under cold running water, dry with paper towels and set aside.

Cut each tomato into 4 pieces and set aside.

Rinse the eggplant under cold running water. Dry with paper towels, peel and dice.

In a food processor, pulse the eggplant and tomato until coarsely chopped. Transfer to a small bowl, add chopped basil, half of the mozzarella, salt, ground pepper and toss gently.

Preheat oven to 375°F.

Stuff portobello caps with filling and top with remaining shredded cheese. Bake until the mushroom caps are soft or until the wonderful smell of this appetizer brings you back to the kitchen from wherever you are in the house, 20 to 25 minutes.

Transfer to a serving plate, garnish and serve hot.

MAKES 6 appetizers
PREPARATION 30 to 40 minutes
GARNISH fresh basil leaves

1 medium eggplant

6 portobello mushrooms

2 medium tomatoes

½ cup chopped fresh basil

½ cup shredded mozzarella cheese

Salt and freshly ground pepper to taste

PREMIUM

Holland America and Princess Cruises are the favorites in this category of cruising that features elegant ships, wonderful entertainment, world-wide itineraries and, of course, some of the best food at sea. Style may be a little more upscale, with people dressing for dinner in the well-appointed, often two-story dining rooms and in the reservations-only specialty restaurants. Passengers are more experienced cruisers with a mix of ages that appears more mature than contemporary cruisers.

These folks definitely take three things seriously: where the ship is going, the size of their stateroom (and whether it has a balcony), and the quality and presentation of the food. The cruise lines in this category focus on the dining experience as a point of differentiation. Personnel have additional training in wines and might appear more attentive by offering a special appetizer not normally found on the menu. Nightly choices will definitely be more varied and the number of choices for appetizer and entrée will be much greater than on board contemporary cruises.

Likewise, *Cruising Cuisine's* selections in the Premium category will generally require a bit more preparation and will offer you the opportunity to be more creative when it comes to presentation. Don't be afraid to use some of these recipes as either a sit-down starter or during a cocktail hour.

RÖSTINI TOPPED WITH SOUR CREAM & CAVIAR

On a Baltic cruise visiting St. Petersburg, I served pancakes with caviar one evening at a cocktail party for American passengers. Later, several guests told me that they thought the combination of a potato pancake with caviar was the hit of the cruise. Remember that caviar can be served on more than one type of pancake, and you'll be a sensation when you pass these hearty hors d'oeuvres featuring red and black caviar.

Thickly shred the potatoes and transfer to a small bowl. Add flour and egg and mix until combined. Season with salt and pepper.

In a large skillet, heat 3 tablespoons of oil over medium heat. Spoon 1 tablespoon of potato mixture into the skillet, making as many mini-pancakes as you have room in the pan until the mixture is gone. Cook until golden brown, about 30 seconds on one side and 10 seconds on the other. Add more oil if necessary.

Transfer mini-pancakes to a paper towel and blot excess oil. Arrange on a platter and let cool.

In the center of each mini-pancake spoon $1/2$ teaspoon of sour cream and top with about $1/2$ teaspoon of caviar. Sprinkle with coarsely chopped chives.

Serve at room temperature.

MAKES 8 to 10 röstini
PREPARATION 20 to 25 minutes
COOKING 3 to 6 minutes
GARNISH 1 tablespoon coarsely chopped chives

2 large potatoes, peeled

1 tablespoon all-purpose flour

1 egg, whisked

Salt and pepper to taste

3 to 4 tablespoons vegetable or olive oil

2 tablespoons sour cream

2 tablespoons caviar

TASTY CHEESE TOASTS

My non-cooking husband thinks I am a genius with this easy recipe that will take only 10 to 15 minutes of your time. The secret is not to tell him or your guests how long it really takes to make this tasty treat!

Preheat large skillet over medium heat. Brush with olive oil and toast the bread slices until nicely browned and crisp on both sides.

In a small bowl, mix garlic and mayonnaise until combined. Spread each piece of bread with mayonnaise mixture and sprinkle with cheese.

Transfer the toasts to a platter and serve immediately.

MAKES 6 toasts
PREPARATION 5 to 10 minutes
COOKING 3 to 5 minutes

1 tablespoon vegetable or olive oil

6 baguette slices, ¼ to ½ inch thick

1 garlic clove, minced

1 tablespoon mayonnaise

½ cup grated Monterey Jack or Swiss cheese

TIP These cheese toasts are also a good accompaniment to soups.

CHICKEN SATAY WITH
SPICY PEANUT SAUCE

If you have cruised in the Far East and Northern Europe, you will not be surprised at the popularity of satay in both areas. The far-flung islands of Indonesia where this dish has its humble beginnings, were first colonized by the Dutch. The bright flavors of freshly ground peanuts, combined with the spicy bite of red pepper, make a fabulous dipping sauce for oriental spiced meats, hot off the grill. This is a mini version of delicious satay served as an appetizer.

In a small bowl, make marinade by combining lemon juice, lime juice, 1 tablespoon of oil, cayenne pepper, curry powder, red pepper and garlic cloves. Place chicken squares in marinade, cover and marinate in the refrigerator for 1 hour.

Heat 2 tablespoons of oil in medium skillet over high heat. Quickly sauté chicken until lightly browned, 2 to 3 minutes. Arrange chicken in a small shallow bowl and spear with skewers.

Reheat peanut sauce thinning with water if needed and pour over chicken skewers.

Sprinkle chicken and sauce with onion bits and serve immediately.

SPICY PEANUT SAUCE In a small sauce pan, combine all ingredients and bring to a boil over medium heat, stirring constantly. Simmer, stirring until the sauce is thick. Cover and set aside.

TIP Give the appetizer an improved flavor and perfect presentation with canned onion bits from your local store. Peanut sauce can be made up to 3 days ahead. Keep refrigerated.

MAKES 4 to 6 servings
PREPARATION 15 to 20 minutes
MARINATING 1 hour
COOKING 7 to 12 minutes
SPECIAL EQUIPMENT 10 to 12 short bamboo skewers or toothpicks
GARNISH 1 teaspoon fried onion bits

1 tablespoon fresh lemon juice
1 tablespoon fresh lime juice
3 tablespoons olive oil
1 teaspoon cayenne pepper
1 teaspoon curry powder
1 teaspoon crushed red pepper
2 garlic cloves, minced
$\frac{1}{2}$ boneless chicken breast, cut in 1 to 1$\frac{1}{2}$ inch squares
1$\frac{1}{2}$ cups Spicy Peanut Sauce (see recipe below)

SPICY PEANUT SAUCE
MAKES 1$\frac{1}{2}$ cups
COOKING 5 to 8 minutes

1 cup natural peanut butter
1 cup water
1 tablespoon fresh lime juice
2 tablespoons soy sauce
1 teaspoon brown sugar
4 garlic cloves, minced
1 tablespoon grated fresh ginger

FILLO SHELLS WITH SMOKED SALMON & LEMON DILL CREAM

As light and tasty as a gentle breeze on a lazy, summer afternoon in the Greek Islands, these delicate fillo shells filled with salmon and lemon cream are perfect for outdoor parties. The shells can be found in the frozen food section of your grocery store, and the hors d'oeuvres can be made up to 3 hours ahead and kept refrigerated prior to serving.

Slice salmon in very thin strips, transfer to a small plate and cover with plastic wrap. Chill in the refrigerator until ready to fill the shells.

Preheat oven to 375°F.

In a small bowl, mix softened cream cheese, lemon juice and dill until combined. Fill each shell with ¼ to ½ teaspoon of mixture.

Transfer filled shells to a baking sheet and bake until the edges are golden brown, 4 to 5 minutes.

Top the filling with ¼ teaspoon of cool salmon strips. Garnish and arrange on a platter.

Serve at room temperature.

MAKES 15 shells
PREPARATION 15 to 20 minutes
COOKING 4 to 5 minutes
GARNISH fresh dill

**3 slices smoked salmon
(Nova or Norwegian)**

2 tablespoons cream cheese

2 tablespoons fresh lemon juice

1 tablespoon finely chopped fresh dill

**1 package mini fillo dough shells
(15 shells in a package)**

CRAB CAKES WITH MUSTARD SAUCE

Whether cruising in Alaska or the Caribbean, I always look for these favorites on the menu as either hors d'oeuvres or presented as a sit-down appetizer. If you prefer a crunchier coating, try Panko, Japanese bread crumbs. Widely available in stores, Panko's crisp, delicate crumb is a perfect contrast to the soft and moist crab interior.

In a medium bowl, mix crab meat with egg, mayonnaise, mustard, Worcestershire sauce, lemon juice, scallions and carrot until combined. Season with salt and pepper.

Using 1 tablespoon of crab mixture, form round, flat cakes. Dip the flat sides in bread crumbs. Arrange on a plate, cover with plastic wrap and chill in the refrigerator for 2 to 3 hours.

In a large skillet, heat oil over medium heat. Sauté crab cakes until nicely browned, about 3 to 4 minutes on each side. Remove cakes from pan and blot excess oil with paper towels.

Transfer to a platter and serve hot with Mustard Sauce on the top or on the side.

MUSTARD SAUCE In a small bowl, whisk all ingredients until combined. Cover with plastic wrap and chill for 1 hour.

MAKES 10 to 12 mini crab cakes
PREPARATION 30 to 35 minutes
CHILLING 2 to 3 hours
COOKING 6 to 8 minutes
GARNISH fresh parsley

1 cup jumbo lump crabmeat

1 egg, beaten

1/2 cup mayonnaise

1 tablespoon Dijon mustard

2 teaspoons Worcestershire sauce

2 teaspoons fresh lemon juice

1/2 cup green scallions, sliced

1 small carrot, shredded

Salt and pepper to taste

3 tablespoons bread crumbs

1/2 cup olive oil

1 cup Mustard Sauce (see recipe below)

MUSTARD SAUCE
MAKES 1 cup
PREPARATION 2 to 4 minutes
CHILLING 1 hour

3 tablespoons Dijon mustard

3 tablespoons mayonnaise

2 teaspoons fresh lime juice

SHRIMP STUFFED TOMATOES

Here is a zesty shrimp appetizer that can be made ahead of time and kept in the refrigerator. The secret is the piquant Thousand Island dressing that tops the shrimp. Your guests will be wowed by both the ease of preparation and the elegance of the presentation.

Cut tomatoes in half and carefully scoop out the pulp. In the bottom of each tomato, layer 1 teaspoon of Spicy Carrots then shrimp to the top. Dollop with 1 teaspoon of Thousand Island Dressing on top.

Arrange one stuffed tomato in the center of each serving plate. Garnish each tomato with fresh dill in the center of shrimp. Serve cold.

THOUSAND ISLAND DRESSING In a small bowl, whisk ketchup, mayonnaise, mustard, pickle relish and lemon juice until smooth. Stir in shredded egg, celery and cucumber. Season with cayenne. Transfer to a small bowl and cover with plastic wrap. Chill in the refrigerator for 1 hour.

MAKES 8 appetizers
PREPARATION 20 to 25 minutes
GARNISH fresh dill

4 medium round tomatoes

$^1/_2$ cup marinated Spicy Carrots (optional)
(see recipe on page 73)

1 package (8 ounces) cooked and peeled salad shrimp

1$^1/_2$ cups Thousand Island Dressing
(see recipe below)

THOUSAND ISLAND DRESSING
MAKES 1$^1/_2$ cups
PREPARATION 10 to 15 minutes
CHILLING 1 hour

$^1/_2$ cup ketchup
$^1/_2$ cup mayonnaise
$^1/_2$ teaspoon Dijon mustard
$^1/_2$ teaspoon sweet pickle relish
1 teaspoon fresh lemon juice
1 egg, hard-boiled and finely shredded
1 teaspoon shredded celery
1 teaspoon shredded cucumber
Cayenne pepper to taste

TIP Serve with toasted bread on the side.

PÂTÉ STUFFED EGGS

These hors d'oeuvres will put the "devil" in traditional deviled eggs. You can make them up to 12 hours ahead and keep refrigerated. For serious liver lovers, the pâté can be served by itself on crackers and sprinkled with finely chopped fresh parsley.

Trim chicken livers, wash and towel dry.

In a medium skillet, heat oil over low heat. Sauté onion and garlic until lightly browned. Increase the heat to medium and sauté chicken livers until golden, 2 to 3 minutes. Add chicken broth and bay leaf and cook until the liquid mostly evaporates, 5 to 6 minutes. Strain the remaining liquid from the livers and remove the bay leaf. Transfer to a small bowl and let cool.

Peel eggs and cut each egg in half lengthwise. Carefully remove the yolks and reserve the whites.

In a food processor, blend the yolks, liver, butter, Cognac, sour cream, salt, pepper and nutmeg until smooth. Transfer to a bowl, cover with plastic wrap and chill in the refrigerator for at least 30 minutes.

Before serving, stuff each egg white with ¹/₂ to 1 tablespoon of pâté. Arrange on a platter, garnish and serve cold.

MAKES 12 hors d'oeuvres
PREPARATION 15 to 20 minutes
COOKING 8 to 10 minutes
CHILLING 30 minutes
GARNISH fresh parsley

¹/₂ **pound chicken livers**

2 tablespoons olive oil

1 small onion, coarsely chopped

1 garlic clove, chopped

¹/₄ **cup chicken broth**

1 bay leaf

6 eggs, hard-boiled

1 tablespoon unsalted butter

¹/₂ **to 1 tablespoon Cognac or brandy**

1 tablespoon sour cream

Salt, pepper and nutmeg to taste

CHAMPIGNON
& ASPARAGUS RISOTTO

Whether cruising the Po River or enjoying the post-cruise memory, freshly prepared risotto is always an elegant first course. My favorite memory of dining in Italy is risotto with asparagus and fresh mushrooms, but you can create your own version by adding tomatoes and basil, mushrooms, scallops or shrimp.

Snap off tough ends of asparagus and discard.

Cut off asparagus tips, approximately 2 inches and set the stalks aside. In a small pot, bring 2 cups of water to a boil and blanch the tips over medium heat until soft, 2 to 3 minutes. Remove from cooking liquid and immediately immerse in ice water to stop cooking process. Drain and reserve.

Cut the stalks in ½-inch pieces, transfer to a plate and set aside.

Heat large sauté pan over low heat, melt 1 tablespoon of butter and sauté champignons, mixing quickly until lightly browned. Remove the champignons and set aside.

In same sauté pan, add olive oil and over medium heat, sauté onions and garlic until softened. Add rice and mix well until coated with oil. Add wine and stir until evaporated, about 1 minute. Add chicken broth and cook until absorbed, stirring often, 3 to 4 minutes. When absorbed, add ½ cup of water and simmer, stirring often, until new liquid is absorbed, 5 to 6 minutes. Add cut asparagus stalks, then about 1 cup water little by little until the rice is cooked and creamy but not soupy nor dry, 14 to 16 minutes. Remove from heat, stir in the mushrooms, Parmesan cheese and heavy cream. Season with salt and white pepper.

In a small skillet, melt 1 tablespoon of butter over medium heat. Quickly sauté the asparagus tips until lightly browned. Set the skillet aside.

Prepare 4 or 6 plates on a working surface. Arrange the cutter in the center of a plate. Fill with risotto and carefully remove the form. Repeat with remaining plates. Top every risotto with warm asparagus tips and sprinkle with Parmesan cheese. Serve immediately.

MAKES 4 to 6 appetizers
PREPARATION 16 to 20 minutes
COOKING 32 to 34 minutes
SPECIAL EQUIPMENT 3 to 4 inch cutter or any other round form without a top and/or bottom
GARNISH grated Parmesan cheese

½ **pound asparagus, washed and trimmed**

5 cups water

2 tablespoons unsalted butter

5 small champignons, sliced

1 tablespoons olive oil

1 small onion, finely chopped

1 garlic clove, finely chopped

1½ cups Arborio (risotto) rice

½ **cup dry white wine**

½ **cup chicken broth**

½ **cup Parmesan cheese, grated**

½ **cup heavy cream**

Salt and white pepper to taste

CRAB DELIGHTS

Serve this light and delicate crab salad either as hors d' oeuvres or as a specialty salad on a luncheon or afternoon tea buffet. Your guests will think they are lounging around the pool deck of a ship that is surrounded by sparkling blue water below and a clear blue sky punctuated only by puffy white clouds above.

In a medium bowl, mix crabmeat together with potato, egg, chives, cheese and mayonnaise. Season with salt and pepper. Chill in the refrigerator for 1 to 3 hours.

Clean cucumbers and cut in 1 to 1$^1/_2$ inch slices. Scoop out the center of each slice and spoon about $^1/_2$ teaspoon of the crab mixture. Garnish and arrange on a serving platter.

BUFFET PRESENTATION Double the recipe. Instead of combining the ingredients as above, layer half of the potatoes in the bottom of a serving dish. Build the salad by layering half of the chives, crabmeat and eggs. Spread $^1/_4$ to $^1/_2$ cup of mayonnaise over the eggs and sprinkle with half the cheese. Continue making layers using the remaining potatoes, chives, crabmeat and eggs. Spread the last layer with remaining mayonnaise and sprinkle with cheese.

Cover with plastic wrap and chill in the refrigerator before serving cold.

MAKES 30 to 36 hors d'oeuvres
PREPARATION 20 to 25 minutes
CHILLING 1 to 3 hours
GARNISH lemon, fresh dill

$^1/_2$ **cup fresh lump crabmeat**

1 small to medium potato, boiled and shredded

1 egg, hard-boiled, peeled and finely shredded

$^1/_4$ **cup chopped chives or green scallions**

$^1/_4$ **cup finely shredded baby Swiss cheese**

$^1/_4$ **to** $^1/_2$ **cup light mayonnaise**

Salt and pepper to taste

3 English hothouse cucumbers

SEA SCALLOP & BACON
HORS D'OEUVRES

"A rose by any other name . . ." There is probably not a cruise ship anywhere in the world that doesn't served bacon-wrapped scallops at some time during the cruise. But I promise that you will think differently about these familiar hors d'oeuvres when you use *Cruising Cuisine's* presentation. Our secret makes the scallop taste better and the bacon stays crisper. Interested? The combination is easy to make and is sure to become your favorite interpretation of this classic.

MAKES 12 hors d'oeuvres
PREPARATION 15 to 20 minutes
COOKING 12 to 16 minutes

12 fresh rosemary sprigs, approximately 2½ inches in length

4 slices of bacon

12 medium scallops

Prepare rosemary spears by cleaning approximately 1½ inches from the bottom of the sprig, leaving the leaves only on the top. Transfer spears to a bowl with cold water and set aside.

Cut bacon strips in thirds and sauté until crisp. Remove and drain on paper towels. Sauté scallops in bacon fat until lightly browned, 1 to 2 minutes on each side. Drain on paper towels.

Arrange scallops on a platter. Top each with a piece of bacon and pierce with a rosemary spear from the top to the bottom. Serve immediately.

SOLE ESCABÈCHE

There are many delicious recipes using sole, but none better than this delicious presentation which properly showcases the delicate texture of the fish and the bright flavors of Spain's famed Costa del Sol. This unusual recipe is sure to become one of your "signature" dishes.

TO MAKE MARINADE In a large pot, dissolve the sugar in water and bring to a boil. Add the bay leaves, peppercorns, salt and garlic. Boil over medium heat for 2 minutes. Remove mixture from heat and add the wine, vinegar and onion rings. Cover the pot and let cool at room temperature.

TO COOK FISH Preheat oil in a large skillet over medium heat until hot. Quickly sauté the filets, making sure you cook only 10 to 15 seconds on each side and do not overcook. Transfer filets to a flat platter or a shallow dish where you will marinate the fish. Let cool.

Pour cold marinade over fish, spreading vegetables and chopped rosemary in one layer. Cover with plastic wrap and marinate in the refrigerator for at least 6 hours and up to 2 days.

When ready to serve, transfer whole filets without marinated spices to the plates, garnish with twisted slices of lemon and fresh rosemary.

MAKES 6 servings
PREPARATION 8 to 12 minutes
COOKING 10 to 12 minutes
MARINATING 6 hours to 2 days
GARNISH 4 thin lemon slices, fresh rosemary

2 tablespoons sugar

4 cups water

2 bay leaves

$\frac{1}{2}$ teaspoon whole black peppercorns

Salt to taste

2 garlic cloves, sliced in half

4 tablespoons dry white wine

4 tablespoons white distilled vinegar

4 medium onions, sliced in rings

3 tablespoons olive oil

6 filets of grey sole

1 teaspoon coarsely chopped fresh rosemary

TIP For added elegance, serve with 3 or 4 cooked and chilled asparagus lightly dressed in vinaigrette alongside the fish.

SALMON WELLINGTON

Cruising in Norway and Sweden, you can't help noticing two things that are in great supply: fjords and salmon. The Scandinavians have more ways to prepare salmon than they have first names for male children! This delicious pastry stuffed with salmon and leeks is versatile beyond belief. Prepare ahead and keep frozen. Then simply bake 20 to 25 minutes before your guests arrive.

In a large skillet, heat oil over medium heat until hot. Add leeks and sauté until light brown. Add white wine and bay leaves and simmer until reduced by half, 2 to 3 minutes. Season with salt and pepper, add dill and stir in lemon juice and sour cream. Set aside and cool. When cold, remove the bay leaves.

Preheat oven to 400°F.

Unfold pastry on a lightly floured surface. Roll out pastry sheet into a 12-inch square. Cut into 12 rectangles, 3 x 4 inches each. Place 1 salmon slice in the center of one half of the rectangle along the shorter edge. Top the salmon with heaping teaspoon of filling. Lightly brush edges of pastry with water. Fold other half of rectangle over the salmon. Firmly press edges to seal. Brush each puff pastry with egg.

Bake about 20 minutes or until golden brown. Transfer to plates and serve immediately.

MAKES 8 appetizers
PREPARATION 30 to 40 minutes
COOKING 24 to 28 minutes

2 tablespoons olive oil

2 leeks, white and light green part sliced

½ cup dry white wine

2 bay leaves

Salt and pepper to taste

½ cup coarsely chopped fresh dill

1 tablespoon fresh lemon juice

1 tablespoon sour cream

½ package (2 sheets in package) frozen puff pastry, thawed

1 medium salmon fillet (4 to 6 ounces) cut in 12 slices, each 1 x 2 inches and ½ inch thick

1 egg, whisked

TIP For a variation, add spinach with or instead of leeks. Prepared appetizers can be made up to 1 week ahead and kept frozen. Simply defrost at room temperature 20 to 30 minutes before baking. Serve with baby greens salad on the side.

BRIE & CHAMPIGNON TARTLETS

Cruising the waterways of France is a wonderful way to experience the varied flavors of French country cuisine. Another winning combination is our recipe for crispy tartlets made with creamy Brie and champignons sautéed in white wine. Whether you chance upon this dish along the Saône, Rhone, or Seine rivers, or sample it in the comfort of your own home, this recipe is sure to evoke wonderful memories.

Thinly slice champignons and set aside.

In a large skillet, preheat oil over medium heat until hot. Sauté onions until lightly golden. Add mushrooms and bay leaves and sauté until lightly browned. Add white wine, salt and pepper. Simmer until the wine evaporates. Remove from heat, discard the bay leaves, and let cool.

Preheat oven to 350°F.

Unfold pastry on a lightly floured surface. Roll out each pie crust into approximately a 12-inch round. From each round cut six 3½-inch rounds and pierce each with a fork in 6 or 7 different places. Place each round in ungreased tartlet form and press the dough to the bottom and to the sides forming a tartlet. In each tartlet, spoon about 1 tablespoon of Brie, filling lower half of the form, and top with about 1 teaspoon of champignons. Sprinkle with a few almond slices and a pinch of brown sugar.

Bake the tartlets until golden and almonds are brown, 15 to 20 minutes. Cool for 2 minutes and remove from forms. Place on a serving platter and serve warm.

MAKES 12 tartlets
PREPARATION 20 to 26 minutes
COOKING 22 to 28 minutes
SPECIAL EQUIPMENT 12 non-stick tartlet forms, 3 inches in diameter

8 ounces (12 to 14) medium champignons

4 tablespoons olive oil

2 medium onions, finely chopped

2 bay leaves

½ cup dry white wine

Salt and pepper to taste

1 package (2 sheets) refrigerated pie crust (Pillsbury or other)

4 ounces Brie cheese, cut in ½-inch squares

¼ cup sliced almonds

1 tablespoon brown sugar

TIP Do not hesitate to use any kind of dough and add a creative touch by using fresh cranberries or chopped pears instead of almond slices.

MEDITERRANEAN SHRIMP COCKTAIL

This recipe is from a chef I met cruising near Portofino, on the Italian Rivera. He made this simple shrimp cocktail special by adding an unusual spiced carrot mixture that is almost an appetizer itself. It gave me the idea that not all shrimp cocktails are created equal and that there is always room for a personal touch. Slice the carrots with a mandolin kitchen slicer and marinate in the refrigerator for at least 6 hours.

In 6 martini glasses, arrange iceberg lettuce on the bottom, top with marinated carrots and place cocktail shrimp around the rim of the glass.

Thinly slice a lemon and cut each slice from the center to the edge. Arrange 2 slices on each glass rim between shrimp.

SPICY CARROTS Slice carrots as thin as possible using a mandolin and reserve in a medium heat-proof bowl.

In a small bowl, combine all spices.

In a small pot, heat the oil over medium heat until almost smoking. Carefully pour hot oil over carrots, add garlic, spices and toss until carrots are evenly coated with oil. Set aside and let cool.

When cold, cover with plastic wrap and marinate in the refrigerator for at least 6 hours and up to 3 days.

MAKES 6 cocktails
PREPARATION 10 to 15 minutes
SPECIAL EQUIPMENT 6 martini glasses

½ cup iceberg lettuce, sliced
2 cups Spicy Carrots (see recipe below)
1½ pound (40 to 46) cocktail shrimp, peeled
1 lemon

SPICY CARROTS

MAKES 2 cups
PREPARATION 20 to 30 minutes
MARINATING 6 hours to 3 days
SPECIAL EQUIPMENT mandolin kitchen slicer

8 large carrots, peeled
1 teaspoon coarsely ground coriander seeds
½ teaspoon chili powder
1 teaspoon dried basil
1 teaspoon curry powder
½ teaspoon sugar
½ teaspoon nutmeg
½ teaspoon black pepper
¼ teaspoon salt
1 cup olive oil
4 garlic cloves, minced

TIP Serve Spicy Carrots with seafood, sausages, and sandwiches or add to fresh salads.

CALF'S LIVER SERVED WITH BACON & ONIONS

Savory calf's liver prepared with crispy bacon and golden onions is almost irresistible as an appetizer or a main course. The delicate liver should be quickly sautéed in hot oil and butter just before serving.

Rinse liver with cold water and pat dry with paper towels. Cut each slice in half. Dip in flour, cover with plastic wrap and refrigerate until ready to cook.

In a large skillet, cook bacon over moderate heat until brown and crisp. Remove bacon with a slotted spoon to a paper towel and blot excess oil, then transfer to a deep plate or a bowl. Cover with aluminum foil and keep warm. Discard all but 3 tablespoons of bacon drippings from the skillet.

Separate onion slices into rings. Lightly dip in flour. Preheat skillet with remaining bacon drippings over medium heat until hot and sauté onion rings until golden. Remove with slotted spoon to a paper towel and drain. Transfer the onions to the plate with bacon and keep warm.

In a large skillet, preheat oil and butter until hot and almost smoking. Sauté liver until cooked and lightly browned, about 1½ minutes per side for medium rare, about 2 minutes for medium well and about 2½ minutes for well done. Do not overcook. Season with salt and pepper.

Transfer liver to 4 serving plates. Arrange bacon and onions on top. Sprinkle with parsley and serve immediately.

MAKES 8 servings
PREPARATION 15 to 20 minutes
COOKING 15 to 18 minutes
SPECIAL EQUIPMENT aluminum foil, approximately 12 x 14 inches
GARNISH ¼ cup finely chopped fresh parsley

8 ounces calf's liver, sliced in ½ inch thick slices

4 tablespoons all-purpose flour

3 ounces (4 slices) bacon

1 large onion cut in ¼ to ½ inch slices

2 tablespoons olive oil

2 tablespoons unsalted butter

Kosher salt and freshly ground pepper to taste

TIP Cooked onions and bacon can be kept in a warm preheated oven, about 200°F to 250°F, for up to 30 minutes.

POACHED SALMON FILET WITH
HERB & HORSERADISH SAUCE

Whole poached salmon, dressed up for a buffet table, is perhaps the most impressive fish presentation on many cruise ships. Borrowing from this concept, _Cruising Cuisine's_ adaptation of this time-honored favorite pairs poached salmon with a piquant herb and horseradish sauce for a tempting appetizer.

MAKE A COURT BOUILLON In a small pot, combine water and dry white wine and bring to a boil. Add sliced carrots, celery, leeks, thyme, bay leaves, black pepper and salt. Bring to a boil and cook over low heat for 20 minutes. Set aside.

Rinse salmon under cold running water and dry with paper towels. Cut each filet in half. Place in the bottom of a sauté pan. (Note that if you poach the whole salmon filet, the pan must be large enough to place the salmon without bending the edges.) Pour the court bouillon and all the cooked vegetables, herbs and spices over the salmon. Bring to a boil and simmer over low heat, covered, for 5 minutes until just opaque in the center. Do not overcook. Remove from the heat and allow the salmon filet to cool in the bouillon completely.

When cold, remove the filet from the bouillon, dry with paper towels, wrap in plastic and chill in the refrigerator for at least 2 hours.

Before serving, transfer the filets to plates. Garnish with lemon and dill. Serve at room temperature or cold with Herb & Horseradish sauce on the side.

HERB & HORSERADISH SAUCE In a small bowl, mix the sour cream and mayonnaise until smooth. Add horseradish and dill and mix gently until combined. Transfer to a serving bowl and serve with poached salmon.

MAKES 6 servings
PREPARATION 20 to 25 minutes
COOKING 30 to 38 minutes
plus cooling
CHILLING 2 to 8 hours
GARNISH lemon, fresh dill, horseradish sauce

4½ **cups water**

1 **cup dry white wine**

3 **medium carrots, sliced in rings**

2 **ribs of celery, sliced in rings**

2 **leeks, white part, sliced in rings**

2 **sprigs of fresh thyme**
(or ½ teaspoon of dried thyme)

3 **bay leaves**

½ **teaspoon whole black peppercorns**

1 **teaspoon salt**

3 **small salmon filets (8 ounces)**

2 **cups Herb and Horseradish Sauce**
(see recipe below)

HERB & HORSERADISH SAUCE
MAKES 2 cups
PREPARATION 2 to 5 minutes

1 **cup sour cream**

1 **cup mayonnaise**

4 **teaspoons horseradish (or to taste)**

½ **cup chopped fresh dill**

TOMATO, MOZZARELLA & BASIL SKEWERS

Don't let the simplicity of this appetizer fool you into thinking it is not for an elegant cocktail party. Your guests will delight in these tasty morsels and never know how hard you worked on them. Be sure that someone manages to drop the hint about "the secret is in the homemade pesto sauce!"

Cut mozzarella into twelve 1-inch squares.

On a frilly toothpick, thread one tomato, one basil leaf and one mozzarella square. Repeat using all ingredients. Dip the mozzarella squares in fresh Pesto Sauce.

Arrange on a platter and serve cold.

PESTO SAUCE Here is a hint about making pesto sauce. Avoid the temptation of using a food processor as the basil leaves will break, turn watery green, and lose much of their delicate flavor. The best way to make pesto is simply chopping the leaves with a knife. Pesto can be made up to 4 weeks ahead and kept refrigerated.

In a medium bowl, gently mix all ingredients until combined. Transfer to a small container and store in the refrigerator.

MAKES 12 skewers
PREPARATION 15 to 20 minutes
SPECIAL EQUIPMENT 12 frilly toothpicks

2 ounces mozzarella cheese

12 cherry or grape tomatoes

12 fresh basil leaves

1/2 cup fresh Pesto Sauce (see recipe below)

PESTO SAUCE
MAKES 1 to 1 1/2 cups
PREPARATION 5 to 10 minutes

2 cups finely chopped fresh basil leaves

2 garlic cloves, minced

1/2 cup grated Parmesan cheese

1/2 cup extra virgin olive oil

2 bay leaves, finely crushed

1/2 cup pine nuts, coarsely chopped

Kosher salt and pepper to taste

MELON & PROSCIUTTO SKEWERS

During my first trip to the Mediterranean, I marveled at the color and taste of the varied array of fresh fruits and vegetables in Italian markets. Italians know that when the flavors are right, there is not a recipe in the world that can improve on nature. They prove the case with prosciutto and melon, an old favorite that blends the sweetness of melon with the subtle flavor of prosciutto. You will enjoy serving this at your post-cruise party when everyone is talking about the diets they are planning now that the cruise is over!

Scoop 12 small melon balls or cut a slice into 12 one-inch squares.

Cut each slice of prosciutto into 3 pieces.

With a frilly toothpick, pierce folded piece of prosciutto and melon. Repeat with remaining ingredients.

Arrange on a serving platter and serve cold.

MAKES 12 skewers
PREPARATION 10 to 15 minutes
SPECIAL EQUIPMENT melon ball cutter (optional); 12 decorative toothpicks

1 slice melon

4 thin slices of prosciutto

TIP For a variation and an impressive presentation, arrange skewers in a martini glass.

LUXURY

Imagine a small hotel that offers everything you could possibly want – fine art and elegant surroundings, large accommodations and suites with sweeping balconies, large walk-in closets, and marble bathrooms. Then compliment the surroundings with attentive and knowledgeable staff available at your call, and food prepared to order in chic and casually elegant venues where you dine when and with whom you wish.

Are you in Beverly Hills or New York? More likely, you are on board one of the luxury Yachts of Seabourn, or on the Italian-built ships of Silversea. Or perhaps you are in the Queens Grill aboard Cunard's legendary Queen Elizabeth 2, or on one of the Radisson Seven Seas' vessels. Wherever you are, don't doubt for a minute that you are staying at one of the finest hotels in the world.

You'll find your traveling companions worldly and sophisticated. They are accustomed to the best – an expectation met nightly with open sitting arrangements at dinner, appetizers and hors d' oeuvres served in suites (or better still, on balconies), and at cocktail parties arranged for a few new friends.

You will be at home among them when your party features recipes from this section. Here you will find innovative ingredients and exciting presentations that will have your guests asking, "When is your next cruise . . . oops, I mean party?"

AVOCADO, SHRIMP & ARUGULA APPETIZER

Imagine you are cruising in the Greek Islands. There is a soft knock at your door and your room steward tells you he has a special treat for you to enjoy on your private veranda before dinner. If the Greek Islands are not in your backyard, create something special with this quick and easy appetizer that does not require any cooking. You can replace the shrimp with fresh crabmeat or marinated scallops and have a totally different appetizer. And remember: the more time you take arranging the plate, the more luxurious it will look!

Finely dice the avocado, transfer to a small bowl, add lemon juice and toss gently.

Place a cutter in the center of a serving dish. Arrange half of avocado on the bottom of the form to make a 'pancake'. If you do not use a form, try to make it as round as possible. Make next layer using half of the shrimp. Arrange shrimp carefully by placing them one by one as you would arrange cooked shrimp on a serving platter. Spoon 1 teaspoon of dressing in the center of appetizer. Top with half of the chopped arugula. Repeat with remaining ingredients.

Sprinkle prepared appetizer with Parmesan cheese and dress with dots of dressing around on plate.

WHITE WINE AND MUSTARD DRESSING In a small bowl, whisk mustard, white wine, vinegar and balsamic vinegar until smooth. Cover with plastic wrap and chill in the refrigerator until ready to serve.

MAKES 2 appetizers
PREPARATION 15 to 20 minutes
SPECIAL EQUIPMENT 3½-inch cutter or any other round form without a top and bottom
GARNISH freshly grated Parmesan cheese

2 ripe Hass avocados, peeled and seed removed

2 tablespoons fresh lemon juice

½ cup cooked and peeled salad shrimp

1 tablespoon White Wine and Mustard Dressing (see recipe below)

1 cup fresh arugula, finely chopped

WHITE WINE AND MUSTARD DRESSING
MAKES about 1 tablespoon
PREPARATION 2 to 3 minutes

1 teaspoon Dijon mustard

2 teaspoons dry white wine

1 teaspoon distilled white vinegar

1 teaspoon balsamic vinegar

SALMON ROLLS

Salmon has been associated as a symbol of luxury since the early days of cruising, when some "experts" used to rank cruises on the basis of how much salmon was displayed on the midnight buffet! Times have changed, but tastes have remained constant, hence this delicate presentation of a favorite. These attractive hors d'oeuvres are sometimes called "pinwheels" for their multi-color, circular shape.

In a blender or food processor, mix cream cheese with garlic and lemon juice.

Place the foil sheet on a flat work surface. Lay a piece of plastic wrap on top. Arrange salmon pieces forming a rectangle in the middle of the sheet, approximately 9 x 11 inches. Spread cream cheese mixture on top of salmon in a thin layer. Sprinkle with fresh dill. Lifting the edge of the plastic wrap, roll the salmon into a tight log like a sushi roll. Carefully remove plastic wrap and roll the log in the foil, giving it a round shape. Chill in the refrigerator for at least 2 hours.

Unwrap the log. Using a very sharp knife, cut into slices, approximately 1 to 1½ inches thick.

Pierce each roll with a frilly toothpick, place on a serving platter. Serve cold.

MAKES 14 to 20 hors d'oeuvres
PREPARATION 15 to 20 minutes
CHILLING 2 to 12 hours
SPECIAL EQUIPMENT 1 aluminum foil sheet, approximately 10 x 12 inches; 1 plastic wrap, approximately 10 x 12 inches (optional); 14 to 20 frilly toothpicks

4 ounces (½ container) soft cream cheese

1 garlic clove, minced

1 teaspoon fresh lemon juice

4 ounces (6 to 8 thin slices) smoked salmon (Nova, Norwegian)

¼ cup finely chopped fresh dill

TIP When rolled in foil, salmon rolls can be kept in the refrigerator prior to serving. They will look fresh if unwrapped just before slicing and sprinkled with fresh lemon juice just before arranging on a platter.

FRENCH CRÊPES

This versatile dish gives you the perfect opportunity to make a lasting impression on your most favored guests. Delight them as you offer two of *Cruising Cuisine's* favorite stuffings: scallop and shrimp in Cognac cream sauce and an exotic mushroom filling. Let your imagination find variations to these favorites or make your crêpes special by garnishing and folding them differently.

In a medium bowl, whisk eggs until blended. Add milk and whisk until combined. To avoid lumps, add flour by sprinkling ¼ cup at a time over the bowl, incorporating well after each addition. Add sugar and salt and mix well. Add water a little at a time, whisking until the batter is perfectly smooth.

Heat pan over medium heat and brush with oil. When very hot, fill about half a ladle with batter and pour slowly around the edge of the pan, rotating quickly so the batter covers the bottom in a very thin layer. Pour excess batter back into the bowl. Cook each crêpe until golden brown, about 30 seconds, then turn over and cook about another 10 seconds.

Transfer to a plate and continue making the rest of the crêpes until all batter is used.

MAKES 20 to 24 crêpes
PREPARATION 10 to 12 minutes
COOKING 40 to 50 minutes
SPECIAL EQUIPMENT 8- or 10- inch round crêpes pan

2 eggs

2 cups milk

3 cups all-purpose flour

½ teaspoon sugar

½ teaspoon salt

2 cups water

TIP Add some flour if the crêpes are too thin and difficult to turn, or add water or milk if the crêpes are too thick.

Crêpes can be made up to 2 days ahead and kept refrigerated until ready to use.

FRENCH CRÊPES FILLING
SCALLOP & SHRIMP
IN COGNAC CREAM SAUCE

MAKES 20 to 24 crêpes
PREPARATION 15 to 20 minutes
COOKING 14 to 16 minutes
SPECIAL EQUIPMENT oven-proof
platter or serving plates (optional)

½ pound (6 to 8) medium sea scallops

2 tablespoons sunflower or vegetable oil

1 tablespoon unsalted butter

1 medium onion, finely chopped

1 garlic clove, finely chopped

½ cup coarsely chopped mushrooms
(baby-Bella, cremini or button mushrooms)

½ pound raw shrimp, if medium or large,
cut in half

1 bay leaf

¼ cup Cognac or brandy

3 tablespoons heavy cream

1 tablespoon finely chopped fresh parsley

½ cup finely chopped green scallions
or chives

1 teaspoon truffle oil

Salt and pepper to taste

24 chives, approximately 4 to 5 inches
in length

Rinse scallops under cold running water and dry with paper towels. If the scallops are large, cut each in half or in quarters.

In a large skillet, preheat oil over high heat until hot. Melt butter and quickly sauté scallops, stirring constantly until lightly golden and not overcooked, 1½ to 2 minutes. Transfer the scallops with oil and juices to a plate and set aside.

In same skillet, add the remaining oil and preheat over medium heat until hot. Sauté the onions and garlic until soft. Add the mushrooms and cook until lightly browned, about 1 minute. Add shrimp and sauté until light pink. Add bay leaf and Cognac and simmer until Cognac evaporates. Add heavy cream and simmer until reduced by half. Add parsley, green scallions and scallops. Stir the mixture and remove from heat. Immediately stir in the truffle oil and season with salt and pepper. Remove the bay leaf.

TO FOLD THE CRÊPES In a small pot, bring water to a boil. Blanch chives about 10 to 15 seconds and transfer into ice water to cool. Spoon approximately 1 tablespoon of filling in the center of a crêpe. Pull up the edges and tie with a chive. Repeat with remaining crêpes.

Arrange assembled crêpes on an oven-proof serving platter or plates and keep in a warm oven (225°F to 250°F) prior to serving, up to 30 minutes.

FRENCH CRÊPES FILLING
SPINACH, GOAT CHEESE & WILD MUSHROOMS

In a large skillet, heat 2 tablespoons of oil over medium heat. Sauté onions and garlic until soft. Add the mushrooms and cook until the liquid from mushrooms has evaporated. Add about 1 tablespoon of oil if necessary, bringing the oil back to temperature. Add half of the spinach. After spinach wilts, add remaining spinach and sauté until reduced in size, about 30 seconds. Add white wine and simmer until reduced by half. Add heavy cream, chives and lemon juice. Stir and remove pan from the heat. Season with nutmeg, salt and pepper and mix with crumbled goat cheese until combined.

TO FOLD THE CRÊPES In a small pot, bring water to a boil. Blanch chives about 10 to 15 seconds and transfer into ice water to cool. Spoon approximately 1 tablespoon of filling in the center of a crêpe. Pull up the edges and tie with a chive. Repeat with remaining crêpes.

Arrange assembled crêpes on oven-proof serving platter or plates and keep in a warm oven (225°F to 250°F) prior to serving, up to 30 minutes.

TIP If you have limited time or you have difficulty folding the crêpes as described above, try a different folding. Simply spoon about 1 tablespoon of the filling in a log form at one edge of the crêpe. Fold the "short" edge over the filling. Roll the crêpe. Repeat with remaining filling and crêpes. Use any left over filling as a topping.

Crêpes can be made ahead, layered with plastic wrap and kept in the refrigerator prior to serving, up to 2 days.

MAKES 20 to 24 crêpes
PREPARATION 10 to 15 minutes
COOKING 10 to 14 minutes
SPECIAL EQUIPMENT oven-proof platter or serving plates (optional)

3 tablespoons sunflower or vegetable oil

1 medium onion, finely chopped

1 garlic clove, finely chopped

1 cup shiitake or chanterelle mushrooms, coarsely chopped

6 ounces fresh spinach leaves, trimmed and washed

¼ cup dry white wine

3 tablespoons heavy cream

¼ cup chopped chives or green scallions

½ teaspoon fresh lemon juice

¼ teaspoon nutmeg

Salt and pepper to taste

4 ounces goat cheese, crumbled

BUTTERFLY SHRIMP IN HERB PESTO

Think of your ship lying at anchor off Sorrento. Add a gentle breeze across the deck. Listen for the sound of happy music floating from the shore. Then taste these delicious shrimp formed in the shape of a butterfly. They may seem to "fly" off the tray as this tasty presentation makes its way around your party.

Peel shrimp leaving the tail intact. Make a cut along the back of each shrimp and remove vein. Wash thoroughly under cold running water then blot with paper towels. Using a very sharp knife, cut through along the back of the shrimp leaving the tail and opposite end not severed. Open each shrimp carefully by holding it with tail up to form a butterfly shape. To get the shrimp to 'stand' for an impressive final presentation, pierce each shrimp through the tail and opposite end with skewers. Repeat with remaining shrimp.

In a medium bowl, toss shrimp with pesto, cover with plastic wrap and marinate in the refrigerator for at least 2 hours for best flavor.

Preheat oven to 400°F.

Approximately 30 minutes before your guests arrive, stand the shrimp on a baking sheet. Bake until pink, 15 to 17 minutes.

Transfer to a serving platter and serve hot or warm.

HERB PESTO In a food processor, chop cilantro, garlic, bay leaves, pine nuts, red pepper, Parmesan cheese and olive oil until coarse. Transfer to a medium bowl. Add basil and lemon juice and mix until combined.

MAKES 16 hors d'oeuvres
PREPARATION 35 to 40 minutes
MARINATING 2 to 24 hours
COOKING 15 to 17 minutes
SPECIAL EQUIPMENT 16 wooden skewers or toothpicks, soaked in water for 45 to 60 minutes

16 (approximately 1 pound) raw jumbo or king size shrimp

1 cup fresh Herb Pesto (see recipe below)

HERB PESTO
MAKES 1 to 1½ cups
PREPARATION 10 to 15 minutes

½ **cup fresh cilantro leaves**

3 garlic cloves

2 bay leaves

½ **cup pine nuts**

1 teaspoon crushed red pepper

½ **cup grated Parmesan cheese**

½ **cup extra virgin olive oil**

¼ **cup fresh basil leaves, finely chopped**

2 tablespoons fresh lemon juice

COCKTAIL MEATBALLS
WITH GREEK OLIVE FILLING

Look for these on your next cruise to the Greek Islands when you venture inland to the smaller villages. This typical taverna fare turns a familiar cocktail party staple into a unique and sophisticated treat. Tiny bites, stuffed with feta cheese and Greek olives will become the hit of the evening. For a variation, you can also use a mushroom, spinach, ricotta or goat cheese filling. They will be talking about your meatballs for weeks to come!

In a small bowl, mix feta and olives. Set aside.

In a medium bowl, combine the ground meat, chopped onions and egg. Add Tabasco, salt and pepper and mix well. Form into 1-inch balls. On a slightly floured work surface, gently flatten each meatball to form a thin round. Place about $\frac{1}{2}$ teaspoon of feta mixture in the center of each round and reform each round into a $1\frac{1}{2}$-inch ball, making sure filling is totally enclosed by meat. Lightly flour.

In a large skillet, heat half of the oil over medium heat. When very hot, sauté meatballs turning until all sides are golden brown. Remove cooked meatballs from pan and drain on paper towels. Continue with rest of meatballs, adding more oil if necessary.

Arrange on a serving dish and sprinkle with chopped parsley.

TOMATO SAUCE In a sauce pan, heat the olive oil over low heat. Sauté the garlic, stirring constantly until lightly golden. Add tomatoes with the juice, bay leaf, thyme and simmer until reduced by half. Set aside and season with salt and paprika. Discard the bay leaf and pour the sauce over the meatballs or into a sauce bowl, if the sauce is served on the side.

TIP Meatballs are best when served freshly cooked and hot with tomato sauce on the side. Prepared meatballs can be made up to 12 hours ahead and kept refrigerated. Sauté until cooked before your guests arrive, transfer to an oven-safe serving platter and keep in warm oven (250°F) prior to serving, up to 30 minutes.

MAKES 20 to 24 meatballs
PREPARATION 30 to 36 minutes
COOKING 10 to 16 minutes
GARNISH finely chopped parsley

3 tablespoons crumbled feta cheese

2 tablespoons chopped pitted Greek olives

$\frac{1}{2}$ pound ground pork

$\frac{1}{2}$ pound ground beef or veal

$\frac{1}{2}$ medium onion, finely chopped

1 egg, beaten

Tabasco Habernero Hot Pepper Sauce (see mail order sources), salt and pepper to taste

$\frac{1}{2}$ to 1 cup all purpose flour

3 tablespoons olive oil

TOMATO SAUCE
MAKES 1$\frac{1}{2}$ cups
COOKING 8 to 10 minutes

1 tablespoon olive oil

3 garlic cloves, minced

1 can (14.5 ounces) diced tomatoes

1 bay leaf

2 teaspoons finely chopped fresh thyme or dried thyme

Salt and paprika to taste

LOBSTER SPRING ROLLS
WITH MUSTARD-SOY SAUCE

Your guests will think they are visiting the Imperial Palace in Beijing's Forbidden City with this treat. The bright spring flavors of the vegetables combined with the succulent sweetness of lobster will become the stuffing of legends. The secret is in the bean sprouts and Savoy cabbage. Spend some time slicing the vegetables julienne-style and carefully fold the rolls making them very firm. Spring rolls can be made ahead and refrigerated or frozen.

In a small covered pan, bring water to a boil and cook whole carrot, celery, garlic, onion and bay leaves for 5 to 8 minutes. Season with salt and add lobster. Boil until cooked, 8 to 10 minutes. Remove lobster, let cool for 5 minutes and remove meat from the shell. Transfer the meat to a plate and let cool. Return the shell to the cooking liquid and simmer, covered, until reduced by half. Remove the pan from the heat and let lobster stock stand for 20 to 30 minutes.

Line a colander with wet cheesecloth. Slowly pour the stock through cheesecloth leaving the shell and vegetables in the pan or colander. Discard everything but stock. Let cool. Chill in the refrigerator or freeze for later use for lobster bisque, fish soup or lobster sauce.

On a cutting board, coarsely chop lobster meat into ¼-inch pieces. Transfer to a medium bowl and gently mix together with cabbage, bean sprouts, carrots, bell pepper and celery.

In a small bowl, whisk the egg and set aside. Place one eggroll wrapper on a work surface and spoon about 1 tablespoon of vegetables in a narrow 3-inch line down the center of the wrapper. Brush open edges of the wrapper with egg. Fold the short edge over the filling and overlap with left and right sides. Roll into a tight and firm roll and press the edge to seal. Repeat with remaining ingredients.

In a deep medium-size pan or deep fryer, fry the rolls until golden brown, 4 to 5 minutes. Drain on paper towels. Cut each roll diagonally and arrange on a serving plate. Sprinkle with sauce and garnish with fresh herbs or vegetables. Serve with Mustard-Soy Sauce on the side.

MUSTARD-SOY SAUCE In a small bowl, make a sauce by combining the water and mustard. Let stand for 10 to 15 minutes. Add soy sauce and sesame oil. Whisk the sauce until smooth and thick. Set aside and cool. Add shallots.

MAKES 9 spring rolls
PREPARATION 45 minutes
COOKING 30 to 36 minutes
SPECIAL EQUIPMENT colander; cheesecloth

1 medium carrot, peeled
1 celery rib
2 garlic cloves
1 small onion, outer skin removed
2 bay leaves
1 teaspoon kosher salt
1 (8 to 10 ounces) fresh lobster tail
½ cup finely sliced Savoy cabbage
½ cup bean sprouts
¼ cup julienne sliced carrots
¼ cup julienne sliced red bell peppers
¼ cup julienne sliced celery
1 egg
1 package (9 sheets) egg roll wrappers
Oil for frying
½ cup Mustard-Soy Sauce (see below)

MUSTARD-SOY SAUCE
MAKES ½ cup
PREPARATION 15 to 20 minutes

½ cup cold water
¼ to ½ cup dry mustard
2 tablespoons soy sauce
Sesame oil to taste
1 tablespoon chopped green shallots or chives

SPINACH MINI-STRUDELS

You'll think your cruise has arrived in Mykonos when you taste our crispy fillo dough with delicate spinach filling. Locally known as 'spanokopita,' this recipe is sure to have your guests pining for a return to the charming waterfront cafés. Fillo is very delicate so don't forget to keep it covered with a moist kitchen towel when assembling the strudels. For a different flavor, add some ground ginger to the spinach filling.

In a large skillet, heat oil over medium heat. Add chopped onion, minced garlic and sauté until lightly cooked. Add half of the spinach and when reduced, add remaining spinach and sauté until wilted, about 1 minute. Add scallions and remove from the heat. Add lemon juice, nutmeg, salt, pepper and allow the filling to cool.

Thaw the pastry sheets in the box for 20 to 30 minutes. While thawing, transfer cooled spinach mixture to a medium bowl and add sour cream, Parmesan cheese and feta crumbs. Set aside.

Melt butter in a small sauce pan over medium heat and set aside.

Carefully remove fillo rolls from package and gently unfold. Immediately cover with damp paper towel to prevent sheets from drying out.

Prepare the strudels using 4 sheets of pastry per strudel. Place the first sheet on a cutting board or waxed paper and cover remaining pastry with damp towel. Brush the sheet with melted butter. Top with next sheet and repeat brushing until all 4 sheets are used. Keep remaining sheets under damp towel while working. Spoon 4 tablespoons of filling along the edge of the sheet in a log form, leaving a 1-inch border at each end of the filling. Fold in the sides over the filling and roll into a loose roll. Brush log with butter. Transfer to a baking sheet. Repeat with remaining sheets and filling.

Preheat oven to 375°F.

Bake folded logs until golden brown, 15 to 20 minutes. Let cool about 5 minutes. Using a very sharp knife, cut each roll into 8 mini-strudels. Arrange on a platter and serve warm or at room temperature.

MAKES 36 to 40 mini-strudels
PREPARATION 50 to 60 minutes
COOKING 30 to 35 minutes

3 tablespoons vegetable oil

1 large onion, finely chopped

3 garlic cloves, minced

1 package (10 ounces) fresh spinach leaves, washed and trimmed

¼ cup finely chopped green scallions

½ teaspoon fresh lemon juice

¼ teaspoon nutmeg

Salt and pepper to taste

1 package (20 sheets) frozen fillo dough pastry

2 tablespoons sour cream

¼ cup grated Parmesan cheese

4 ounces traditional feta cheese, crumbled

2 tablespoons unsalted butter

SHRIMP & ROSEMARY RISOTTO

One of the inside secrets of this cruising category is a term called "a la minute," generally meaning food cooked to order. In the galley of small luxury ships, or in alternative dining rooms aboard larger vessels, a la minute preparation is what sets luxury cruising apart from the rest. Nowhere is this more evident than in this delicate risotto dish that uses fresh rosemary to create a wonderful highlight to the sweet shrimp. Served as an appetizer, the resulting dish is unforgettable.

In a large skillet, heat 2 tablespoons of olive oil over medium heat. Sauté shrimp, garlic and bay leaves, mixing constantly until the shrimp are light pink, 2 to 3 minutes. Season with salt and pepper. Place the shrimp on a plate and set aside.

In a large sauté pan or stockpot, heat 2 tablespoons of olive oil over medium heat. Sauté onions until lightly cooked. Add rice and mix well until coated with oil. Add 1 cup of water and stir constantly until absorbed. Add wine and continue stirring slowly until evaporated. Add broth, ¹/₂ cup at a time until absorbed, stirring the rice constantly, 12 to 14 minutes. Add one rosemary sprig and remaining water a little at a time until the rice is cooked and has a creamy texture, 11 to 12 minutes. Remove from the heat and discard the rosemary. Stir in heavy cream, Parmesan cheese and shrimp. Season with salt and pepper.

Transfer to plates, sprinkle with Parmesan cheese and garnish with rosemary sprigs. Serve immediately.

MAKES 10 to 12 servings
PREPARATION 10 to 15 minutes
COOKING 35 to 40 minutes
GARNISH 10 to 12 rosemary sprigs, freshly grated Parmesan cheese

4 tablespoons olive oil

1 pound raw jumbo shrimp, shelled and deveined

2 garlic cloves, finely chopped

2 bay leaves

Salt and pepper to taste

1 medium onion, finely chopped

3 cups arborio (risotto) rice

4 cups water

1 cup dry white wine

3 cups fish or chicken broth

1 rosemary sprig

¹/₄ cup heavy cream

¹/₂ cup Parmesan cheese

TIP For a variation, add saffron powder dissolved in hot broth which will give your risotto a beautiful color.

SESAME ENCRUSTED TUNA BITES

These tasty hors d'oeuvres had its origin as the "sesame seared tuna" made famous as a restaurant entrée. Our recipe is both elegant and simple, and will please your most sophisticated guests. Try this "show stopper" the next time those sophisticates are talking about the most recent cruise that you weren't on!

Cut tuna steak into small 1- inch squares and season with salt. In a small bowl, mix white and black sesame seeds.

In a large skillet, heat the oil over medium heat until hot. Dip each piece of tuna into the mixed seeds until all sides are covered. Quickly put each piece in the heated skillet and turn them, letting each side fry for a few seconds. The tuna should be rare in the middle, so be careful not to overcook. Place cooked pieces on a paper towel to blot excess oil and then transfer to a serving platter.

Serve at room temperature with frilly toothpicks and Wasabi-Soy Sauce on the side.

WASABI SOY-SAUCE In a small serving bowl, whisk soy sauce and wasabi paste to taste.

MAKES 18 to 20 hors d'oeuvres
PREPARATION 6 to 10 minutes
COOKING 1 to 3 minutes

10 to 12 ounces tuna steak

Salt to taste

3 tablespoons white sesame seeds

3 tablespoons black sesame seeds

3 tablespoons vegetable oil

Wasabi-Soy Sauce (see recipe below)

WASABI-SOY SAUCE
MAKES 1 small sauce bowl
PREPARATION 1 minute

4 tablespoons soy sauce

Wasabi paste to taste

SEARED TUNA CANAPÉS

This variation on our sesame encrusted tuna recipe transforms the presentation to an unexpected surprise. It is perfect for dressier parties when guests are reluctant to "dip and drip!" With the addition of spicy cream cheese, the flavor is more delicate than the usual wasabi hot sauce.

Season tuna with salt and coat all sides with sesame seeds.

In a large skillet, heat the oil over medium heat until hot. Cook tuna quickly in the heated skillet and turn, letting each side sear for a few seconds. The tuna should be rare in the middle, so be careful not to overcook. Transfer tuna to a paper towel, blot excess oil and transfer to a cutting board. Let cool.

While cooling, whisk cream cheese and wasabi paste in a small bowl until combined.

Slice room temperature tuna steak in 12 thin slices, about ¼ inch thick.

Spread each cracker with cream cheese mixture and top with one slice of tuna.

Arrange on a platter, garnish and serve cold.

MAKES 12 canapés
PREPARATION 18 to 20 minutes
COOKING 1 to 2 minutes
GARNISH 12 cherry or grape tomato halves, 12 parsley leaves

6 to 8 ounces tuna steak

Salt to taste

2 tablespoons white sesame seeds

2 tablespoons vegetable or olive oil

1 tablespoon cream cheese

Wasabi paste to taste

12 square crackers

SEAFOOD MARTINI

We have identified several ways that luxury cruising cuisine is different, including advance preparation, fresh and interesting ingredients and, most importantly, presentation. While this recipe meets the definition of luxury on several levels, the presentation can be the creative hit of any party by using your most elegant stemware. This dish improves with time, so marinate seafood at least 6 hours ahead. *Bon appétit!*

Rinse raw seafood under cold running water before preparing. Cook the seafood before marinating.

SCALLOPS Preheat skillet over medium heat until hot. Add olive oil and sauté scallops until lightly colored, about 1 minute on each side. Do not overcook. Drain on paper towels. Set aside to cool.

MUSSELS Bring water to a boil and add mussels. Boil until the shells pop open. Remove the mussels with a slotted spoon to a bowl. Do not use if shell does not open. Set aside to cool. Remove mussels from shells.

CALAMARI/SHRIMP Bring water to a boil and add calamari or shrimp. When water returns to a full boil calamari or shrimp are done. Using a slotted spoon, remove from the water to a plate or bowl. Let cool.

SALMON Preheat oven to 375°F. Place salmon on a piece of foil. Sprinkle with dry white wine and olive oil. Fold as an envelope and bake until cooked, 15 to 20 minutes. Unfold and let cool.

MAKE MARINADE In a medium bowl, mix the olive oil, vinegar, bay leaves, garlic, lemon juice and Herb Mixture. Add seafood and gently toss. Refrigerate for at least 6 hours and up to 2 days before serving.

Serve marinated seafood in attractive martini glasses. Arrange sliced lettuce on the bottom and top with 1 tablespoon of seafood. Garnish each seafood martini with lemon slice and fresh dill.

MAKES 10 to 12 martinis
PREPARATION 5 to 10 minutes
GARNISH 12 lemon slices, fresh dill

1 pound of your favorite fresh seafood (scallops, mussels, shrimp, calamari, salmon etc.)

½ cup extra virgin olive oil

2 tablespoons distilled white vinegar

3 bay leaves

3 garlic cloves, sliced in half

2 tablespoons fresh lemon juice

2 tablespoons of Herb Mixture

HERB MIXTURE

½ teaspoon lemon zest

¼ teaspoon dry onion (or ½ fresh onion, sliced)

1 tablespoon fresh or dried dill

¼ teaspoon dill seed

1 teaspoon jalapeño pepper

¼ teaspoon salt

MUSSELS À PROVENCE IN TOMATO, GARLIC & WHITE WINE SAUCE

This marvelous appetizer will remind your cruise guests of their time in the romantic ports of Cannes, Nice, and Monte Carlo. The fabulous flavors of Provence combine with those of the Riviera creating a dish that is both aromatic and tasty. Your menu will heat up if you use a chafing dish to serve the mussels accompanied with fresh baked or toasted bread for dipping in this heavenly sauce!

Remove the skin from the tomatoes and finely dice the pulp. Transfer to a small bowl and set aside.

Rinse mussels under cold running water and set aside.

Bring water to a boil and add mussels. Boil until the shells pop open. Remove the mussels with a slotted spoon to a bowl. Do not use if shell does not open.

In a large skillet, preheat olive oil over medium heat. Sauté chopped onions and garlic until lightly cooked and golden. Add diced tomatoes and sauté until the liquid from the tomato has evaporated. Reduce the heat if necessary. Add white wine and simmer until reduced by half. Add bay leaves, lemon juice and sour cream. Stir gently and season with salt and ground pepper. Set aside until ready to serve.

Arrange cooked mussels in deep serving plates. Generously ladle hot sauce over each mussel. Serve immediately.

MAKES 4 servings
PREPARATION 10 to 15 minutes
COOKING 20 to 26 minutes

2 medium tomatoes

2 pounds (26 to 30) mussels

3 tablespoons olive oil

1 small onion, finely chopped

6 garlic cloves, finely chopped

2 cups dry white wine

2 bay leaves

1 tablespoon fresh lemon juice

1 teaspoon sour cream or heavy cream

Salt and freshly ground pepper to taste

TIP To easily remove the skin of a tomato, make a small X at the bottom that only slightly breaks the skin. Dip in boiling water for 10 to 20 seconds. Remove with a slotted spoon and drop into ice water.

LOBSTER & CRAB CAPPELLETTI
IN PISTACHIO & GARLIC SAUCE

What can be better than freshly made pasta? Several ships in the luxury category feature fresh pasta every day. We think our recipe for this delicate appetizer is better than any you might take home from your next cruise.

TO MAKE DOUGH On a wooden surface, sift flour making a mound. Form a well in the center. Carefully crack the eggs into the center and add salt, oil and herbs. With your fingers, and without letting the eggs spread on the working surface, combine the eggs with a little flour from the edges of the well. Add more flour into the center and mix until combined. Knead the dough until all the flour is used and the dough is firm and elastic, 10 to 15 minutes. Add more flour if the dough is sticky. Transfer the dough to a bowl and sprinkle with flour. Cover with plastic wrap and set aside while preparing the filling.

TO MAKE FILLING In a small bowl, mix lobster, crabmeat and chives until combined.

TO MAKE CAPPELLETTI BY HAND Unwrap the dough and cut into 4 pieces. Work with one piece at a time. Lightly sprinkle a large work surface with flour. Flatten the dough with the palm of your hand. Sprinkle again with flour and roll into a very thin layer, as thin as possible, approximately 5 inches in diameter. Using a sharp knife, trim the edges to make a square. Cut each square of dough in 2-inch strips. Cut each strip into 2-inch squares. Spoon about 1/2 teaspoon of filling in the center of each square. Fold each square in half making a triangle. Press to seal the edges. Brush the edges with water if difficult to seal. Repeat with remaining squares. Arrange triangles on a flat surface or wooden board and sprinkle with flour. Cover with plastic wrap and keep refrigerated while working with remaining dough.

(Continued on page 112)

MAKES 10 to 12 servings
PREPARATION 90 to 120 minutes
COOKING 20 to 24 minutes
SPECIAL EQUIPMENT sifter
GARNISH freshly ground Parmesan cheese, pistachios and fresh oregano leaves

2 1/2 cups all purpose flour

3 eggs

1/2 teaspoon salt

1 tablespoon olive oil

1/2 cup finely chopped fresh herbs (parsley, dill, basil, coriander)

1/2 lobster tail, meat removed and chopped

1 cup crabmeat

1/2 cup chopped chives or green scallions

Salt and pepper to taste

TIP The dough can be made a day ahead and kept in plastic wrap in the refrigerator. Remember to take some extra time because the longer you knead the dough, the better the quality.

LOBSTER & CRAB CAPPELLETTI
IN PISTACHIO & GARLIC SAUCE

TO COOK CAPPELLETTI In a pasta pot, bring a large quantity of salted water to a boil over high heat. Add cappelletti all at once and stir immediately. When the water returns to a boil, stir again and simmer over medium heat until the cappelletti float to the top and al dente, about 3 minutes.

Drain and transfer to a bowl. Immediately mix with Pistachio and Garlic Sauce. Arrange on plates, garnish and serve at once.

PISTACHIO AND GARLIC SAUCE In a large skillet, melt butter over low heat and sauté mushrooms until lightly golden. Add garlic and white wine and simmer until wine has almost evaporated. Add heavy cream and simmer until reduced by half. Add cornstarch and simmer until thick. Add coarsely chopped pistachios and remove from heat.

TIP If cappelletti is made ahead and frozen, cook 1 to 2 minutes longer than instructed in the recipe.

PISTACHIO AND GARLIC SAUCE
MAKES 4 to 5 cups
COOKING 5 to 7 minutes

1 tablespoon unsalted butter

3 cups fresh small wild mushrooms
(sliced in half or quarters if large)

6 garlic cloves, minced

1 cup dry white wine

2 cups heavy cream

2 teaspoons cornstarch

1/2 cup to 1 cup pistachios, coarsely chopped

Salt and freshly ground pepper to taste

SMOKED TROUT WITH SAGE & HORSERADISH

This tasty, smooth topping has its roots in the cool climates of Northern Europe. Serve on crackers or toast points with sliced English hothouse cucumber for a treat straight from the Scottish Highlands. Either way, this taste of the northern climes will have your guests doing a Highland Fling.

In a food processor, blend the trout, mayonnaise, cream cheese, sage, lime juice and horse-radish until smooth. Combine with chopped onion.

Spoon about 1 teaspoon of the mixture on a cracker or slice of cucumber. Repeat with remaining mixture.

Arrange on a serving platter and sprinkle with ground pepper and chives. Serve cold.

MAKES 16 to 20 hors d'oeuvres
PREPARATION 10 to 14 minutes
GARNISH ½ cup chopped chives

1 filet (4 ounces) boneless smoked trout

1 tablespoon mayonnaise or sour cream

1 tablespoon cream cheese

1 teaspoon dried sage

1 teaspoon fresh lime juice

2 teaspoons prepared horseradish

1 small onion, finely chopped

16 to 20 round crackers or English hothouse cucumber slices, ¼ inch thick

Freshly ground pepper to taste

TIP Prepare the mixture up to 6 hours ahead and keep refrigerated until ready to serve.

SMOKED SALMON WITH CAPER CREAM & CAVIAR

Salmon, one of *Cruising Cuisine's* favorite ingredients, is wonderful when combined with caper cream and caviar. For something different and a little out of the ordinary, try blending salmon, capers and cream cheese in a food processor and serve on crackers as a tray-passed hors d'oeuvres. A different presentation of familiar flavors!

In a food processor, blend the cream cheese, sour cream, capers and lemon juice until smooth. Keep one tablespoon of the caper cream in reserve.

Cut each salmon slice in half.

Spread about ¹/₂ teaspoon of caper cream on each cracker. Arrange smoked salmon on the cracker. Spoon ¹/₄ teaspoon of the reserved caper cream on top of the salmon. Place a little caviar on the cream and garnish with fresh dill.

Arrange on a serving platter and serve cold.

MAKES 12 hors d'oeuvres
PREPARATION 10 to 15 minutes
GARNISH 1 tablespoon lemon zest or chopped fresh dill

2 tablespoons softened cream cheese

1 tablespoon sour cream

2 tablespoons capers, drained

1 teaspoon lemon juice

6 thin slices smoked salmon (Nova or Norwegian)

12 round or square dill or water crackers

2 to 3 tablespoons caviar

SALMON & FOIE GRAS NAPOLEONS

Sometimes two very different ingredients can come together to create new taste sensations. This elegant appetizer is a sublime example of how disparate ingredients combine into ultra luxurious Napoleons. Best when made up to 24 hours ahead of time and served on an elegant platter in combination with salmon rolls.

With a sharp knife, cut refrigerated foie gras or pâté in slices as close as possible to the thickness of the salmon.

On a work surface, place a foil sheet and arrange one piece of salmon in the middle. Top the salmon with one slice of the foie gras. "Build" your appetizer by alternating one piece of salmon, then one piece of the foie gras and continue alternating ending with salmon on top.

Wrap the appetizer in foil and chill in refrigerator for 2 hours before cutting.

When ready to serve, remove the foil and cut into ½-inch slices. Dip the knife in hot water after each cut.

Arrange slices on a serving plate, garnish with cucumber or serve with lettuce, endive leaves or baby greens on the side and sprinkle with olive oil and balsamic vinegar.

MAKES 6 to 8 appetizers
PREPARATION 30 to 35 minutes
CHILLING TIME 2 to 6 hours
SPECIAL EQUIPMENT 1 foil sheet, approximately 12 x 14 inches

5 ounces foie gras (or pork pâté with truffles), chilled before using

12 ounces smoked salmon (Nova or Norwegian), cut in thin slices, about ¾ inch thick

TIP Salmon and Foie Gras Napoleons can also be served as hors d'oeuvres if sliced in smaller pieces, placed on crackers and arranged on a serving platter or tray. Garnish each hors d'oeuvre with fresh dill and cranberry.

COOKING TIPS

Before chopping an onion, dip the knife in cold water. It will help prevent your eyes from watering.

To rid the bitter taste in onion, soak sliced onion in cold water for about 15 minutes or until ready to use.

Add a few drops of lemon juice or vinegar to freshly made salad. It will help retain the vitamin C.

To get the maximum juice from a fresh lime, roll it back and forth on a work surface pressing firmly with the palm of your hand before juicing.

To get the maximum juice from a fresh lemon, soak the lemon for 5 minutes in hot water before squeezing.

To keep lemons fresh for a few weeks, store lemons in the refrigerator in closed glass jars filled with fresh cold water.

Keep cleaned vegetables covered with a damp kitchen or paper towel. Do not keep them in water; they will lose their vitamins.

It is recommended that you allow cooked vegetables to cool before making a salad and do not combine cold and warm vegetables. This will help keep your salad fresh for a longer period of time.

After working with vegetables, dip your hands in warm water mixed with vinegar. The natural color of your skin will return and your hands will feel soft and fresh again.

Do not store warm or hot food in the refrigerator. Let it cool first. Vegetables, sauces as well as other foods will lose their vitamins and go bad faster than usual.

Wilted lettuce, dill or parsley will look garden fresh if soaked for about 15 minutes in warm or cold water mixed with 2 to 3 tablespoons of vinegar.

In order to keep herbs fresher longer, store them in plastic bags and do not wash them until you are ready to cook or use them for garnishing.

Do not keep cooked vegetables in boiling liquid. They will become watery and unsavory.

To quickly peel tomatoes, dip them in hot or boiling water for 10 to 20 seconds. You may also use this method for removing skin from sausage before slicing.

Add tomatoes, tomato paste or juice at the end of cooking. They have acid that slows down the cooking process.

Fresh pesto blackens with air,
therefore pour a thin layer of olive oil
after each use or mix a little yogurt
into freshly made pesto.

To remove pâté from a package or
can, hold the unopened package under
very hot running water. Then simply
turn the package over and shake; the
pâté will slide out.

To slice pâté without breaking, dip
the knife in hot water after each cut.

**To save the fresh look of smoked
salmon**, sprinkle it with fresh
lemon juice.

**To determine the freshness of
an egg** do the following: dissolve
one tablespoon of salt in a large glass
of cold water and place the egg in
the glass. A fresh egg will sink: if not
fresh, it will float.

To boil eggs with a cracked shell,
add salt to the boiling water.

To prevent an egg from cracking
while boiling, prick the large end
with a needle.

**After chopping onion, garlic or
working with fish**, your hands may
have a very unpleasant odor. To remove,
rub your hands in salt and wash under
cold running water.

When poaching or boiling fish
do not add fish to cold water; wait
until the water is boiling.

After opening canned tuna or
any canned fish, immediately transfer it
to a glass or plastic container. Do not
refrigerate it in the original can.

**Always thaw frozen seafood in
the refrigerator**; never at room
temperature.

**After chopping onion, garlic or
working with fish**, your hands may
have a very unpleasant odor. To remove,
rub your hands in salt and wash under
cold running water.

**Unlike meat, fish loses its original
taste** when reheated.

**For perfectly soft and juicy calf's
liver**, salt the liver after sautéing.

GLOSSARY

ARUGULA

Or rocket, has long green leaves and strong nutty flavor. It is very popular in Europe and used mostly mixed with other greens in salads. Buy only fresh arugula with firm and green leaves. Sprinkle the leaves with cold water, place in a plastic bag and store in the refrigerator. Use within next 2 days.

ASPARAGUS

Firm and green stalks and tightly closed tips indicate the freshness of asparagus. Unwashed asparagus should be placed in a plastic bag in the refrigerator and used within the next few days. Before cooking the precious tips of asparagus, snap off tough stalk ends letting them break naturally. White asparagus with hollandaise sauce is very popular as a first course in Europe.

AVOCADO

Green avocados are irreplaceable in appetizers, dips or salads. The velvety flesh contains oil that can reduce cholesterol. If avocados are hard, store them in a warm dark place for 2 or 3 days to ripen. To prevent the flesh from darkening after peeling, sprinkle immediately with fresh lemon or lime juice.

CAVIAR

Beluga – large, light to dark grey eggs. Beluga is the finest, most expensive caviar.

Osetra – grey, light or dark brown eggs. This caviar has a refreshing nutty flavor. It is less expensive than Beluga and preferred by many chefs.

Sevruga – small, dark grey to black eggs. Sevruga has a buttery, strong and salty taste. As a low salt alternative, Sevruga malossol is widely available.

CHAMPIGNONS

Champignon is a French word for button mushroom. They can be used for appetizers and main courses, or be chopped and eaten raw in salads. When you buy champignons, make sure that the stems are as white as the caps and that the caps are not bruised. Wash champignons just before cooking.

CILANTRO

Also called coriander, Chinese or Mexican parsley. Cilantro leaves look similar to parsley but are lighter green. The taste is grassier and slightly soapy. Cilantro leaves or seeds are widely useful in Asian, Spanish and Mexican cuisines. Cilantro tends to be very sandy, therefore wash well before using. Keep cilantro in the lower part of the refrigerator rolled in damp paper towels to retain freshness.

EGGPLANT

Dark purple eggplant contains bitter juices that should be drained by salting the flesh and letting it stand for 25 to 30 minutes. Simply rinse with cold water and dry with paper towels before cooking. As with most vegetables, eggplant should be refrigerated in a plastic bag and used within a few days.

FOIE GRAS

Foie gras, is the fattened liver of specially fed and farm raised geese or ducks. There are several types of foie gras:

Raw liver – should be firm, light pink and may be kept vacuum-packed in the refrigerator for up to 7 days.

Fresh foie gras – can be found in terrines, vacuum-sealed packages or cloth. Fresh foie gras is thoroughly cooked and has a soft and creamy texture. It can be kept in the refrigerator for up to $3^1/_2$ weeks and is ready to be served.

Semi-cooked foie gras – has a buttery and little firmer texture than fresh foie gras and is available in terrines, tins or jars. May be stored for up to 6 months.

Preserved foie gras – is thoroughly cooked and has a creamier texture than fresh or semi-cooked foie gras. It can be stored for a few years and becomes creamier as it ages.

Before serving, foie gras should be chilled for several hours in the refrigerator, taken out fifteen minutes before serving, cut thinly with hot knife and served on chilled plates. Foie gras is a main source of a monounsaturated fatty acid that can help protect the cardiovascular system.

KALAMATA OLIVES

The most popular Greek olives these long-shaped Kalamata olives have a purplish black color. They are rich and tasty and can be found in tins or jars in every local supermarket.

LEEKS

Particularly popular in French cuisine, leeks should be bought when the green leaves look fresh and the white root is firm. Keep unwashed leeks in the refrigerator in a plastic bag and use within three days. When ready to use, cut off dark green part, trim the root and rinse properly in cold water. In order to insure that the dirt and sand are washed out, you may want to cut the leeks first and then wash it properly.

MELON

Whether your recipe calls for sweet, green honeydew melon or juicy, orange cantaloupe, melon makes wonderful hors d'oeuvres when paired with cheese or prosciutto. To buy melon, follow your nose!

PORTOBELLO MUSHROOMS

These mushrooms have a large, dark brown cap, very short stem and very rich flavor. Portobellos are very good if grilled or roasted and wonderful if added to appetizers, salads or sandwiches. Make sure to remove the stem, clean the gills and rinse under cold running water before cooking.

PROSCIUTTO

Salt-cured and air-dried, prosciutto originally came from Parma, Italy. When used for hors d'oeuvres and appetizers, prosciutto should be sliced transparently thin. Do not discard the fat that holds all the flavor.

SHIITAKE MUSHROOMS

These delicious light brown mushrooms are tasty and especially healthy because they are low in fat and calories, an excellent source of protein, and can help reduce cholesterol.

SPINACH

This is one of those ingredients that taste differently depending on the way you serve it. When you buy spinach, look for crisp, firm and perfectly green leaves. Unwashed spinach should be stored in a plastic bag in the refrigerator and used within the next few days. Rich in vitamins, deep green leaves are delicious if raw in salads, as well as sautéed, or added to pasta.

TRUFFLE OIL

White or black truffle-flavored olive oil can be found in many supermarkets and is particularly popular in Italian cuisine. Do not let the price scare you away. The small bottle will last a long time. Just a few drops will make a huge difference if added just before serving toasted bread, crackers, risotto, spaghetti or even grilled meat!

RECOMMENDED TRAVEL AGENCIES

Ambassador Tours
cruise and land vacations

717 Market Street
San Francisco, CA 94103
Phone: 415-357-9876
Toll Free: 800-989-9000
Fax: 415-357-9877
www.ambassadortours.com

LANDMARK TRAVEL

12 SE 8th Street
Ft Lauderdale, FL 33316
Phone: 954-523-0727
Toll Free: 800-547-0727
Fax: 954-523-0732
www.Landmark-Travel.com

MAIL ORDER SOURCES

PACIFIC PLAZA IMPORTS, INC.
2870 Howe Road, Suite110
Martinez, Ca 94553
Toll Free: 888-888-4470
www.PlazaDeCaviar.com
PRODUCTS: freshest caviar from Russia and Iran. Plaza de Caviar has shipped to the White House in the past. Imports smoked salmon from Scotland, foie gras from France, truffles from France and Italy and saffron from Iran and Spain.
SHIPPING: via Federal Express next day delivery.

GERMAN DELI
500 North Kimball Avenue
Southlake, TX 76092
Toll free: 877-GERMANY (877-437-6269)
www.GermanDeli.com
PRODUCTS: over 1,500 imported German and European food products including Bratwurst and specialty meats; International spices, seasonings, oils, vinegars, and condiments.
SHIPPING: via FedEx, UPS and Postal Service.

MO HOTTA MO BETTA
P.O. Box 1026
Savannah, GA 31402-1026
Toll Free: 800-462-3220
www.mohotta.com
PRODUCTS: best hot sauces; BBQ and salsas; snacks and spices.
SHIPPING: via UPS Ground Service.

MARKET OF DELICACIES
MARCHÉ AUX DELICES
New York, NY 10028
Toll Free: 888-547-5471
Fax: 413-604-2789
www.auxdelices.com
PRODUCTS: white and wild asparagus; fresh portobello, shiitake, maitake, crimini, enoki and oyster mushrooms; truffles.
SHIPPING: via FedEx next day delivery or UPS Ground Service.

CHEESE EXPRESS
104 Bronson Street, Suite 1
Santa Cruz, CA 95062
Toll Free: 888-530-0505
Fax: 830-423-2096
www.cheeseexpress.com
PRODUCTS: domestic and international cheeses.
SHIPPING: via UPS.

INDEX

RECIPES
Elena Vakhrenova

FOOD EDITORS
Mary Ellis
Andrea Corman

COPY EDITOR
Natasha Mullin

CONSULTING EDITOR
David Gevanthor

PROOFREADERS
Mary Ellis
Andrea Corman
Karen Cozzi

FOOD STYLIST AND PHOTOGRAPHER
Elena Vakhrenova

COVER AND BOOK DESIGN
Bonnie Carter
Adworks of Boca Raton, Inc.
www.adworksagency.com
info@adworksagency.com
888.394.3355

PHOTOGRAPHIC CONSULTANT
Doug Castanedo
Doug Castanedo Photography
www.hotelphotography.com
888.276.0123

PHOTO CREDITS
Page 10 - Courtesy of Carnival Cruise Lines.
All rights reserved.
Pages 44, 124 - Courtesy of Star Clippers.
All rights reserved.
Pages 8, 9, 45, 82, 83 and Back Cover -
Courtesy of Cunard Line. All rights reserved.

Cruising
Cuisine
For Home Entertaining, Inc.